so now he speaks again

so now he speaks again

FRANK E. BUTTERWORTH

ABINGDON PRESS

NEW YORK   NASHVILLE

SO NOW HE SPEAKS AGAIN

Copyright © 1963 by Abingdon Press

Library of Congress Catalog Card Number: 63-7477

SET UP, PRINTED, AND BOUND BY THE
PARTHENON   PRESS,   AT   NASHVILLE
TENNESSEE, UNITED STATES OF AMERICA

DEDICATION

To the multiracial people of Hawaii Nei
through whom God spoke to me so often
in the warmth of their "aloha"
and in the sincerity of their devotion

introduction

I HAVE BEEN FRANK BUTTERWORTH'S BISHOP FOR TEN YEARS. I have had the privilege of appointing him to the First Methodist Church of Honolulu, Hawaii, and to the First Methodist Church of Pasadena, California, during that time. This has given me an opportunity to observe his work at close hand and to hear the reactions of laymen to his preaching. For a number of years he has had his sermons mimeographed, and I read them with such profit that I urged their publication. It is a personal satisfaction to have somebody follow my advice, and I feel sure that those who read this book will be grateful both to the author and the publisher.

Dr. Butterworth's preaching is sharp and clear. No one ever has to wonder what he said or what he meant. His sermons are clearly organized with no murky, obscure generalities. He does not wander out through the brush but walks on the straight path of clear thinking. His wide reading gives him illustrations which are always fresh and never trite. He does not shun the local situation and his congrega-

7

tion is reminded constantly of a need for the Gospel's application just outside the door. I have been impressed with his ability to make the eternal principles march down Main Street.

I enjoy this man's grasp of the social implications of Christianity and his refusal to make the sermon comfort only. Yet he has the true shepherd's concern for the individual which shines through all his preaching. Personal experience and social holiness are held together in a fine balance. It is a great moment when a man has his first book published. That I should be asked to share in this experience has pleased me very much. I introduce you to *So Now He Speaks Again* with the expectation that a great many readers will be as pleased with it as I am.

GERALD H. KENNEDY
Bishop, The Methodist Church
Los Angeles Area

contents

1
a hankerin' to go

Text: Gen. 12:1-9

HAVE YOU TALKED WITH A TEEN-AGER RECENTLY? DID YOU find him to be rather restless, discontented, anxious to get away from home? Year after year many of the finest young people leave home for an education or for a job, not because life at home is unattractive, but because "a hankerin' to go" seems to be ingrained in the adventurous spirit of youth. Comparatively few of us have lived out our lives in the places in which we were born. Census statisticians tell us that the average American moves every five years. Some of this transiency is due to our own increasing employment by corporations, but most of us have migrated simply because of this "hankerin' to go."

Did you ever cross the Cumberland Gap in the Appalachian Mountains and think about that stream of trappers, traders, and settlers who streamed across that notch in the mountain? First in a tiny trickle and finally in a rushing stream, they left behind a life of comparative security on the Atlantic seaboard and moved into the West to seek

11

what they believed to be a larger and fuller life. "A hankerin' to go" is a longing that has spoken to every pioneer. It spoke to Abraham, the father of the Hebrew people, as he dwelt in comparative security in the rich valley of the Euphrates River. Something lured him onward around the Fertile Crescent toward the "promised" land of Canaan, and the stopover at Haran was unable to deter him from the urge to continue into the unknown even at the advanced age of seventy-five.

It was this "hankerin' to go" that caused my great grandparents to bundle up their family and belongings, set out on a creaking sailing vessel, and live on hardtack and sowbelly for six months on the treacherous voyage from England around the Horn and on to New Zealand where they settled as pioneers. What though the Maori tribes beat their war drums, and alarms were periodically sounded from the bell in the schoolhouse on the hill? They found a broadening of soul in migrating to this new land, even as did my grandparents in the days of the gold rush, and my wife's parents who migrated from Sweden in the nineteenth century.

There is "a hankerin' to go" that has led every pioneer into a better land and a better life. To many of them it seemed like a calling—like the voice of God himself. And so now he speaks again to every restless spirit.

The Voice of God May Speak Through Our Discontent With Things as They Are.

Most of us are inclined to look upon discontent as an evil thing. In its right place, however, it may well become

12

the voice of God. Difference of opinion about this has given rise to two quite different religions in our world. Gautama Buddha, after much meditation, came to the conclusion that most of the misery in our world is occasioned by wanting something we cannot have. Therefore, he believed, the way to find peace of mind and utter tranquility in this life is to desire nothing and to be content with things that come your way. In diametric contradiction to this Buddhist passivity were the words of Jesus of Nazareth: "I came that they may have life, and have it abundantly." "Ask, and it will be given you," he promised, for Jesus believed that discontent could lead us to divine discovery. Abraham, too, was discontent with the lack of adequate opportunities in his neighborhood. He had already moved once—from Ur of the Chaldeans to Haran. He had grown rich in flocks and herds at Haran, and if the supposition that he tarried there to please his father is valid it would not be without good reason. Yet the fact remains that many a young man has been held back from achieving his own dreams because of the conservatism of his parents. It is a significant thing that Abraham was not able to achieve his ultimate desire of moving on to Canaan until he was seventy-five years old! He simply wanted more room for his family and for his flocks. He had "a hankerin' to go," and it seemed to him to be the prodding and the promise of God for a better life for himself and for his descendants.

Now the Lord said to Abram, "Go from your country and your kindred and your father's house to the land that I will show you. And I will make of you a great nation, and I will bless you, and make your name great, so that you will be a blessing. I will bless those who bless you, and him who curses you I will curse; and by you all the families of the earth will bless themselves."

So Abram went, as the Lord had told him; and Lot went with him. Abram was seventy-five years old when he departed from Haran. (Gen. 12:1-4.)

Observe how readily these words might be spoken to the Plymouth Pilgrims or to the ancient Hawaiians who migrated in giant canoes across the Pacific from islands far to the southwest. Why should any of these people have moved? They left security behind in favor of uncertainty, and it did not seem to make sense. Yet in each case it was born of a need to move on in order that future generations might enjoy a finer way of life. It took persecution to prod the Pilgrims into moving. It may have taken hunger or volcanic explosions on their native islands to prod the ancient Polynesians, but the "hankerin' to go" was in every case a promise of a better land.

God does not always speak to us in a soft voice. Sometimes his voice sounds harsh, for the "hankerin' to go" may be a response to adversity and hardship. The cliff dwellers of the old Southwest were America's first displaced persons. They were forced to migrate down into the mesa country by drought farther north. The "wandering Jew," the Chinese in dispersion, the successive waves of European immigrants to our country, and the refugees who have brought tremendous talents and contributions to the

American way of life—all these came out of dire poverty. They did not exactly want to come, to leave behind familiar friends and familiar ways in the homeland, but out of fairness to their children they came to keep faith with tomorrow, and see what wonderful things God has done with their progeny!

Think of the many European immigrants who climbed from poverty to leadership after they scrambled to shore on the eastern coast of the United States. We think of Edward Bok and of hundreds like him. An equally significant rise to leadership occurred among the Oriental peoples who approached our shores from the west. If the desperate poverty of China and Japan had not driven their parents to migrate to Hawaii as agricultural laborers around the turn of the century the American Congress would be without the distinguished leadership of Daniel K. Inouye and the American Senate would never have received into its membership Senator Hiram L. Fong. It was not only Negro slaves like Booker T. Washington who rose up from nothingness. One has but to visit the plantation camps on the outer Hawaiian Islands to discover one laborer's cottage after another in which have been reared sons and daughters who have made significant contributions in medicine, engineering, nursing, teaching, and many other walks of life. It was Bishop Charles H. Brent, the first missionary bishop of the Philippines, who once said, "The world's work has always been done by men who have suffered pains or taken pains!" Call it a famine, call it economic necessity, call it the voice of God—but behold how God prepares better things for us by our divine discontent! Arnold J. Toynbee,

15

the twentieth century's great historian, talks, in *A Study of History*, about the "stimulus of blows." He says, "the greater the challenge the greater the stimulus." He shows how this principle has worked in the recovery of certain leaders and peoples as they have been beaten down by some adversity. His point is that a heavy blow can set into motion reactions which will result in greater successes than if there had been no blow at all.

Many of us fail to find life a bed of roses. By scrambling upwards from the thorns we have made a life for ourselves and for our children that is far better than any we have known before. "A hankerin' to go" has been for us the voice of God—sometimes harsh and unpleasant to hear, but disciplining us into a more mature and worthwhile life. So now he speaks again, to us as to Abraham of old—by our divine discontent.

The Voice of God May Speak to Us Through Our Curiosity to Cross the Unknown Horizon.

The urge to explore is a divine implantation within us. The little boy wants to explore a cave. The youth wants to experiment with a motor, with a new theory, or with the chemicals in a laboratory. Mature explorers and researchers give us the elements of human progress. In his fascinating book *The Hunger Fighters* Paul de Kruif tells the story of the aroused curiosity of scientists who pursued their restless inquiry until they discovered ways of halting the hidden hungers of our bodies for vitamins. One of them, Harry Steenbock, de Kruif calls "the Sun Trapper." He had read that a Dutchman sent pigeons to a nervous death when he fed them only on polished rice. He read that a Pole cured such sick pigeons by feeding them only on husks of rice. A Norwegian had found that guinea pigs fed only on grain got sore gums and their teeth dropped out. A British Navy man kept scurvy out of his crew with lemon juice. Norsemen cured sore mouths with raw potatoes and spruce tea, and Norwegian fisherfolk dosed babies with cod liver oil in the winter. Yale professors found that the sore eyes of malnourished rats could be cured with cod liver oil. All these facts piqued Steenbock's curiosity. A laboratory chemist at the University of Wisconsin, he began experiments on goats and eventually suspected that cod liver oil and sunlight could contain the same element. He switched to experimentation on rats and found that undernourished rats could catch growth from their sunbathed companions. He found that hog food which was insufficient for growth became sufficient when basked for ten minutes in the rays of a sunlamp. He fed four rats on food exposed to sunlight and found that they trebled their weight in seven weeks. He had trapped the sun! He found that other foods exposed to ultraviolet light gave the same growth qualities as cod liver oil. The whole industry of vitamin-enriched foods which we have today was born of the curiosity of this Wisconsin chemist leading him in his laboratory to cross the unknown horizon.

Among us we meet those with "a hankerin' to go" down untrod trails—those willing to experiment with the unknown to find for us and our children a promise for the future.

An elementary music supervisor was visiting in a classroom where the children were singing "America the Beautiful." She chanced to pass one child who was singing her own impression of the words: "Oh, beautiful for space ships' skies!" This is a commentary on our age: That even little children today are thinking in terms of the conquest of space. What a thrill it is to be living in an age in which little children can talk seriously about space travel instead of relegating it to the fantasies of science fiction or the comic books! Are we ready for space? Or do we still need to explore new trails in human relations? Must we conquer cancer? Have we plumbed the depths of the human mind and personality? Have we learned how to live together as nations and how to use our enormous technical progress for lifting the burden from the back of the common man? There are still vast unexplored areas for the human mind to chart. There is still a promised land beyond the horizon which daring spirits need to find by the kindling of their curiosity.

Don't try to stop the person with "a hankerin' to go," for you may be trying to muzzle the voice of God! After all, as once he spoke to Abraham through a sense of curiosity about the land beyond the border, so now he speaks again.

It Is Better to Be a Displaced Person Than a Misplaced Person.

If you have "a hankerin' to go" down a way untrod, you may be refusing to listen to the voice of God if you refuse to harken to the voice of your innermost heart.

In Rodgers and Hammerstein's *The Sound of Music* the Mother Superior in the convent sings a wonderful piece of advice to the postulant Maria who has left the convent because of her love for a man. She is advised:

> Climb ev'ry mountain, ford ev'ry stream,
> Follow ev'ry rainbow, till you find your dream! [2]

Age is no excuse! Abraham was seventy-five years of age when God whetted his appetite to move on into a new country. Many a person has begun a second career at retirement. He may have been deterred for awhile due to the pressures of family life from realizing the skill or rendering the public service to which he always felt called. Retirement came as a new lease on life, an opportunity to do the things so long undone and to realize the ultimate destiny of one's self.

Perhaps you have always wanted to paint. It may be that you have had a secret yearning for years to work with children or to identify yourself with some great social cause. No matter how hard you have tried to run away from this longing it has pursued you ruthlessly. "The hound of heaven" keeps baying at your heels, and there is a note of dissatisfaction in your life because of its emptiness in some unfulfilled compartment. Listen to the longing of your soul! As God spoke to Abraham who had tarried too long in the lush valleys of Haran so now he speaks again to those of us who have refused to pay attention to the tugging at our souls. It is not too late. It was not too late for Abraham! If we will give ourselves to the noblest dream that we pos-

[2] Copyright © 1959 by Richard Rodgers and Oscar Hammerstein II. Williamson Music, Inc., New York, N. Y., owner of publication and allied rights.

sess, our children, like Abraham's will rise up to call us blessed. "To your descendants I will give this land," God said to Abraham. Did he not make the same promise to the Pilgrims at Plymouth? Has he not made it to the pioneers who have dared to move out in new directions in every area of life?

So now he speaks again to each and every one of us. When we have the "hankerin' to go" it is time to rise up and follow him.

2

here we go 'round the blackberry bush

Text: Exod. 2:11-15; 3:1-12

AN OUTLAW HAS TO LIVE WITH HIS MEMORIES. AT EVERY
prison there is a substantial number who have brooded
upon their memories. They have not only relived the
pangs of their crimes many times over, but they have likewise brooded upon their misfortune until they believe that
all manner of injustices have been done to them and the
world is against them. This is one way in which an outlaw
may react to his memories—the neurotic way of thinking
about himself. The other way is that which Moses followed
during his years in Arabia as a fugitive from justice. That
was the way of thinking not about himself but about the
sufferings of the people of his own race which had caused
him to commit murder and to be forced to flee from Egypt.
That thought still tormented his mind.

Then something happened! He had lived for sixty years
in the desert, and as an old man of eighty he was leading

the flock of his father-in-law westward in quest of better pasture. Before him loomed Mount Horeb, the sacred mountain of his wife's tribe. Up there on the higher slopes there was precipitation and the grass was more abundant, so Moses began the ascent with his flock toward greener pastures. As he climbed Mount Horeb a tremendous conflict was going on within his soul. Alone in the wilderness he had little company but his memories. Those memories turned back to his years as a child in Egypt when he was reared as a prince and provided with the finest Egyptian education at the priestly college at On. Naturally he had contracted some of the religious ideas of the Egyptians during those formative years of his life. He had learned from the Egyptian priests how to do a few "magic" tricks. He had also shared their interest in monotheism, which led Ikhnaton to insist that the sun god was the one true deity. At the same time, however, he was aware of his Jewish heritage, and the more he beheld of the slavery of his own people the more he wondered about the God of his fathers who would permit such suffering. Furthermore, he had married a Midianite girl whose father was a tribal priest and who believed that the "sacred" mountain which he was climbing was the dwelling place of their tribal gods. What was Moses supposed to believe?

His religious confusion was not unlike that of an Oriental student in an American university whose family is Buddhist and whose teachers and companions are Christians. He can see so much good in both religions that he becomes most confused in attempting to make a choice. It was in this frame of mind that the religiously confused Moses climbed

Mount Horeb with his flock. Then he noticed an unusual sight. By the side of the trail he thought he saw a bush burning yet not consumed, and in that sight of the burning bush, however you may try to explain it, he beheld a parable of the Hebrew people who had been under fire for so long but yet had not been destroyed. As he brooded over his memories and his confusion there came to him a Voice. Perhaps it was not one which could have been recorded on a sound tape, but that it spoke to his mind and heart is proved by the all-out commitment of the closing years of his life to the service of his own people. In that moment Moses felt called of God to be his instrument of deliverance for the suffering Hebrews.

Elizabeth Barrett Browning echoes that same wonder in her lines from "Aurora Leigh":

> Earth's crammed with heaven,
> And every common bush afire with God;
> But only he who sees takes off his shoes,
> The rest sit round it and pluck black-
> berries.

God Spoke to Moses Through the Sufferings of His Fellow Men—And so Now He Speaks Again.

Commuter trains had rolled through the slums of London for many years, and millions had gazed out of the windows at the poverty and misery of the tenement districts. But nobody saw a burning bush! Every commuter was engrossed in his own newspaper or in his own thoughts. Then one day a prosperous young English girl, Muriel

23

Lester, looked out the train window at the familiar scene and for the first time saw something unusual in it. The longer she gazed at the misery of the masses the more she began to wonder what right she had to abundance when these others had nothing. This was her burning bush experience—this was when she turned aside to consider what she saw in a new light and to find it in a calling. The result was the construction of Kingsley Hall and the launching of one of the greatest Christian lives of our generation.

Robert Raikes in Gloucester gazed upon children playing in the streets who could not understand the ritual of an adult church service and for the first time saw in their childish paganism a call to action. That was his burning bush experience, and the first Sunday school came into being. So now he speaks again. A young Chinese returned to Shanghai after his education in an American university. His name was Colonel Thomas Tchou. Many times before he had beheld the cheapness of human labor in his native China and it had not deeply disturbed him. This day, however, as he gazed down upon the dock for the first time he noted the plight of the ricksha-men. Under a Shanghai city ordinance at that time there were only 10,000 licensed rickshas permitted on the city streets. Monopolists bought up this limited number and rented them out to the poor coolies for one dollar a day. A man can only make himself a beast of burden for about eight hours a day; consequently the owners were able to rent out the rickshas on shifts to about 30,000 wretched ricksha boys whose fares barely paid the rent that was charged to them. Thomas Tchou was now educated in economics, and their misery stirred him to do something about it. He succeeded in amending the ordinance to require licenses for the pullers as well as for the owners. This at least restricted the number and protected the licensed pullers. Then he organized the coolies into a trade union to bargain with the owners, and so was able to lift the load of misery from their backs. So now he speaks again through the sufferings of men to those whose eyes are opened to them.

"I have seen the affliction of my people . . . and have heard their cry . . . I know their sufferings, and I have come down to deliver them." This was the voice of God that came to Moses. Was God announcing or calling? Was he speaking of his own intent apart from agents, or was he asking for instruments through whom to work? When you drove to church Sunday morning past children playing in the streets and observed that their costume and their activities both indicated that they were unlikely to receive any religious instruction for another week, were you beholding a burning bush or were you just beating around the bush? Did you click your tongue and say what a pity it was that those children will grow up pagan, or did you arrange this week to fill your car with other people's children? Did you volunteer to teach in the church school or to lead a youth group or a Cub pack? "Only he who sees takes off his shoes, the rest sit round . . . and pluck blackberries." Many of you have been overseas in military service. While in other lands did you see human need, or did you see only pleasure and the tourist sights? Navy men refer to certain ports as "good liberty ports." Does this imply personal pleasure therein for the visiting sailor, or is there ever a thought for the plight of the people who live there and what we as a nation can do to raise their standards?

When you chose your vocation which bush attracted your gaze, the bush that burned with a challenge or the bush that was heavy with blackberries for the plucking? So now he speaks again to us in the cries of our brothers— if we will stop to look and to listen.

God Spoke to Moses in a Moment of Wonder—And so Now He Speaks Again.

When Giuseppe Mazzini was asked what he would have taught in the public schools of Italy he replied, "Some knowledge of astronomy, for one has learned nothing unless he has learned to wonder." God reveals himself only to those who wonder. Dr. Jonas Salk would never have discovered the polio vaccine had he not learned first to wonder. Now he is wondering about cancer, and God may speak to his fertile mind again through this same curiosity. Moses moved from mere sightseeing ("I will turn aside and see this great sight") to awe and worship ("And Moses hid his face"). How many tourists there are who see the surface sights but never have a deeper awakening from what they see. They can tell you all about the beauty spots and the night spots, but they are not in the slightest stirred by historical shrines nor moved by the struggles of a people. They can ride along the magnificent fjords of Norway and talk of nothing but their coffee and their bed covers. They can journey to Hawaii and be fascinated by the hula girls but never sense the drama in the life of the cane cutters on the plantations as they struggle to put their children through college.

Many of us are like the Indiana lad who went to Washington on one of those special trips for teen-agers. He climbed the Washington Monument, visited the Lincoln Memorial, and saw the endless list of inspiring things in the nation's capitol. When his parents asked what he enjoyed most he replied, "Pillow fights!" Can we say much more of thousands of adult Americans traveling abroad today? God speaks to the inquiring mind and to the reverent spirit. "Only he who sees takes off his shoes." None other senses that he is on holy ground.

God Spoke to Moses When He Put Himself at God's Disposal—And so Now He Speaks Again.

Moses was not asked to do anything on his own. He was asked only to keep himself available as an instrument for God's power. He did not have to bring back "the golden fleece" as a test of his ability. God burned the bush; all Moses had to do was to observe it. He didn't even have a match! Here is the flaw in our alibis for not doing more significant things with our lives. We always apologize with the statement that we are weak or are not good enough, forgetting that it is God and not we who will take the initiative if we will but make ourselves available to him.

"Who am I that I should go?" asked Moses. "I am slow of speech and of tongue." Moses tried to avoid responsibility for doing anything about the need which he had beheld. He reasoned that he was not sufficiently talented. He reasoned that he was not good enough. But who said anything about being "good enough" to do the work of God? Do not forget that Moses was a murderer— an outlaw and a fugitive from justice. Yet it was to him that God issued His call! None of us has committed so heinous a crime. It was to the denying Peter that Jesus committed the task of founding the church. It was to Paul the persecutor that God committed the first missionary work. His demand is not for perfection but for willingness to allow oneself to be used of him to minister to the needs of his people.

Dr. Leslie Weatherhead tells us how the father of Sir Hubert von Herkomer was persuaded to spend his last years with his distinguished son. The father, also a sculptor, asked for clay that he might while away the evenings at modeling. Hampered by age and enfeeblement, his fingers were no longer subtle with the clay, and his eyesight was failing. Each night the old man would put aside his work almost in despair, for he could not make what he wanted to make of it. After the father had gone off to bed, however, his son, the master sculptor, would work secretly at the clay. In the morning the old man would look at his work of the previous night and, never knowing that another hand had touched it, would exclaim with delight, "Why it isn't as bad as I thought!" That is what God did with the apparently jaded-out life of Moses, and that is what he can do for you and for me.

So now he speaks again—if we see the call in the world around us and stop simply going round the blackberry bush!

3
asleep—but not in peace!

Text: I Sam. 3:1-18

SAMUEL HAD A JOB, SO TO SPEAK, IN THE TEMPLE, AND EACH
night he slept beside the ark of the covenant which con-
tained the sacred relics. He was in the Temple, but we can
hardly consider him to be of the Temple, for at this point
he was too young to have yet taken much interest in religion and was actually employed in the Temple only because
his mother had taken him there to fulfill a vow she made
when she prayed for a boy child. In that respect Samuel was
not much different from many junior-high-age boys today,
who if asked why they come to church would frankly reply,
"Because my mother makes me!"

At this age a boy begins to daydream and to wonder about
what his role is going to be in life. It is the age of hero
worship, and doubtless young Samuel often dreamed of
himself in various roles as he dozed beside the altar. It was
on such a night—when he was asleep, but not in peace—
that God called to him in the hours just before dawn when

the oil in the altar lamp burned low. He thought he heard his name, and he rose hastily and reported to the old high priest Eli, who was sleeping on the other side of the ark. The old man aroused but denied that he had called the boy and told him to go back to sleep again. Three times this experience was repeated, and after the third time the old man perceived that through the boy's wondering about his future God was now calling him to a responsible life of leadership.

There are several things which we have to notice about this story of the boy Samuel. It parallels and yet contrasts with Jesus' experience in the Temple at the same age. We note that God had to beg for Samuel's attention, while Jesus responded much more readily. We must be cautious about taking this story too literally, for the scriptural account itself uses the term "word" and "vision" interchangeably, although we know that there is a difference between that which is audible and that which is visible. The most important thing to note in this story is its implication concerning the manner of a "call" from God.

There appeared in the New Yorker a few years ago a humorous story entitled "The Presbyterian Call System." It was written by a Presbyterian minister's son and described the fear in which he lived as a teen-ager lest he might receive the "call" which his father often talked about and for which the boy suspected that his mother secretly prayed. There is much confusion in the minds of religious folk concerning the way in which God calls us. Peter Marshall called it "the tap on the shoulder"; others describe it as a "nudge from God." Perhaps a careful examination of the boy

Samuel's call will help us to discover ways in which God tries to help us to find and do his will.

God Had to Call Samuel Repeatedly—And so Now He Speaks Again.

Very few of us recognize a divine urge unless it persists. A classic bit of advice handed out to young men who are thinking about entering the ministry is to say "Stay out of the ministry if you can—but if you just can't silence the inner compulsion that leaves you dissatisfied with anything short of full-time work for the church, then the ministry is for you!" Certainly this was true of my own experience. God had to call me repeatedly before I recognized his bidding. If anyone had told me when I was in high school or in college or even two years after I was out of college and in business that I would ever stand in a pulpit as a Christian minister I would have laughed him to scorn. My original interest in the church was the normal interest of any young person who had grown up in the Sunday school and the youth groups. As the months and the years wore on, however, it gradually became obvious to me that I enjoyed my work in the church more than any other kind of work, and that I was more interested in people than in the details of business transactions. The customer interested me much more than the invoice, and a trip to the Orient finally convinced me that there was a vitality in the Christian message which alone was adequate to transform human society. Through all those years God had been trying to show me that my interests and talents lay in the direction of the

31

ministry, but not until he had called me repeatedly did I realize who was calling.

Bill Suzuki, a young layman, built up a tremendous youth program at the Harris Memorial Methodist Church in Honolulu. Until he was thirty he worked only as a commercial artist. When he took on a group of junior-high youngsters as a counselor he did not recognize a professional calling from God; it was just a bit of part-time volunteer service to the church and to the neighborhood. As the six years of his work with that group went on, however, and he gave an increasing amount of time to these young people and their problems he began to see that he had a larger interest than commercial art. Bill took half a day off work and drove across the Pali to Camp Kailani to talk to me about his future. He was beginning to wonder if he ought to let his vocation and avocation trade places, but the required schooling seemed long and forbidding. It was not until two years later that Bill Suzuki resigned from his position with the city and county of Honolulu and at the age of thirty enrolled as a freshman at George Williams College in Chicago to become a Y.M.C.A. secretary. It took the repeated calling of God over a six-year period to win this dynamic young youth worker.

A young man of my acquaintance was so full of music that he gravitated to a piano as naturally as tacks find a magnet. He could not believe that music was his calling, however. People told him it didn't pay enough! Yet through all the years of his college work and his military experience he found his greatest satisfaction in the composing and playing of music, and it took all those years of repeated calling to enable him to find himself in this field.

You can't hush up the truth about your destiny. A boy on a work camp one summer had a genius for working with little children. As soon as he walked into the room the children rushed to him, for no one else could tell stories so effectively or play with them so tirelessly. He is still the idol of every kid in the neighborhood. What is he doing? Is he wasting his life at a bench in an aircraft factory—or is he waiting to yield to the persistent knock? His destiny will surely find him out some day.

In every large church there are churchmen who grew tired on the job back home and who now seek oblivion in a large fellowship. They are tired of teaching Sunday school. They are tired of going to choir practice every week. They are tired of serving on the church board. One day, however, there will come a word of challenge that they cannot resist, and the born teacher will find himself in a classroom and the born singer again in the choir, for inborn talents and appetites can never be long dormant.

A. J. Cronin, who wrote *The Keys of the Kingdom*, never intended to write. He wanted to be a physician, but after his medical education—like the bald-headed barber—this physician suffered a breakdown in his health and in his convalescence chanced upon his hidden calling. He turned to writing to while away the hours and became one of the eminently successful literary men of our time. James Whistler never intended to paint. He wanted a military career and won an appointment to West Point, but he flunked a course in chemistry. "If silicon had been a gas, I would have been a Major General," remarked Whistler. The day he left West Point was the day the real decision of his life was reached, for it was then that he took up the brush and became famous. You cannot hush up the truth about your destiny.

So now he speaks again—and again! How many times does he have to repeat this inner urging that will not be silenced before we recognize the true calling that is built into us?

God Needed an Interpreter for His Call to Samuel—And so Now He Speaks again.

It took the experience of old Eli to recognize Samuel's call. Quite often it takes the insight of a more experienced person to interpret and understand the urgings of our own hearts.

Think of the talent that might have gone to waste in young Frederick Chopin if it had not been for his music teacher who saw and awakened in him his potential genius. Was it not Anne Sullivan who "called" forth the genius of Helen Keller? How many great athletes have been literally found by their coaches? How many teachers and employers have been instruments used of God to bring out leadership skills in pupils or employees?

Elizabeth Blackwell, the first woman medical doctor in the United States and a celebrated pioneer in medical science, had the idea of becoming a doctor first suggested to her by a woman friend who was dying of a malignant disease. "I have often wondered," the friend said, "why women, who are always preoccupied with the care of the sick, are not allowed to become physicians. If I could have been treated by a woman physician perhaps my illness would have been better understood." The young Blackwell girl replied almost indignantly that she hated everything connected with the body and couldn't bear the sight of a medical book. Her friend died shortly after that, and the memory of their conversation began to haunt Elizabeth and finally to challenge her.

We may be God's interpreter to provide encouragement to someone else's genius. The most significant thing that I will ever write may be a check to contribute toward a scholarship for someone of infinitely more ability than I. The most memorable words I ever speak may be not a public utterance but words spoken in the privacy of a study or a living room in challenging someone else to utilize his talents to the uttermost.

Blessed is the interpreter who alerts someone else to listen for the voice of God. Some years ago in Redlands, California, a beloved educator died. Herbert E. Marsh had served as dean of men at the University of Redlands for many years. To his funeral came scores of persons who had been awakened to a discovery of their own capacities through a simple visit with Dean Marsh. This is the real role of every teacher, of every counselor, and of every parent, not to dictate but to discern and to sensitize, even as Eli tried to help Samuel understand what was happening within himself. So now he speaks again—through those who know both us and him.

The Genuineness of God's Call to Samuel Was Proved by Its Moral Integrity—And so Now He Speaks Again.

Many urges come to us out of the darkness, but God's voice is validated by the degree to which it sounds like him. We will receive much advice and many different promptings in many different directions. How are we to know which advice and which promptings represent the voice of God?

"It is the Lord," said Eli—even though the news which Samuel brought to him was bad news. Young Samuel hated to tell the old priest what God had said, but when compelled to do so he informed Eli that the Lord considered him a failure as a father and that because of the dereliction of his sons his household could not continue the religious leadership of Israel. Eli recognized that however bad this news was, at least it was just, and because God is just it must represent the voice of God.

How can the Lord lead two people in opposite directions? I know of a man who went to see his pastor because he claimed that the Lord wanted him to run for president of the United States! If God had intended that man to run for president he would have prompted the people to nominate him—He would not have prompted the man to nominate himself. We can distinguish the true from the false leadings by the way in which they square away with the nature and moral integrity of the creator himself. So now he speaks again—through our highest and most godlike impulses.

A businesswoman came to see me one day. She said, "I

came to Hawaii because I grew tired of the squirrel-cage existence in a mainland city. I did very well in business there. I made lots of money. But I want to get something more out of life than a paycheck, and I have come here to start over again and to try to find a life of service. Can you direct me to such a field?" That woman was following the lead of her highest impulses, and so she was responding to the voice of God.

The only satisfying basis for a vocational choice or for the proper choice of any given course of conduct is to do the thing that is consistent with the highest and most god-like urging that comes to us. Then we can cry with Eli, "It is the Lord!"

There were two who slept by the altar in the Temple, but only one awakened. Not everyone who sits in the sanctuary can hear the voice of God, but only those who are listening for the repeated urgings, for the interpreted urgings, and for the highest urgings of their hearts. Have you deafened yourself to the voice of God, or have you heard that voice and failed to recognize it?

4

tearing the wings off an angel

Text: II Sam. 12:1-15

SOMEWHERE IN A MUSTY CLOSET IN ALMOST EVERY CHURCH there is a pair of angel wings. Probably they were stored away after a little blond child wore them in a Christmas pageant. Where did we get the notion that angels have wings? Certainly we did not get the idea from Jacob's wrestling partner in the story recorded in the book of Genesis. Neither did it come from the New Testament account of the "young man . . . dressed in a white robe" whom the women saw seated inside the tomb of Jesus on Easter morning. Throughout the Bible an angel is a messenger of God, and the angel was usually human and male in the Old Testament and completely devoid of wings.

God spoke of old through messengers, and so now he speaks again. Let us tear the wings off an angel and see how one of these messengers of God really works. And let us use Nathan as our specimen!

38

"And the Lord Sent Nathan to David."

It is possible so to paralyze the conscience that God can get no impulses through. David was in precisely this position. Although an otherwise godly man, he had beheld a beautiful woman whom he wanted for his harem and had arranged to send her husband, who was one of his faithful soldiers, to the front line of combat so that he was killed, making it perfectly legal for David to marry his wife. Apparently it never crossed David's mind that he had done wrong. He was the king; he gave a command and was obeyed by a professional soldier. He never sensed that he had done wrong in the sight of the God whom he served.

It is easy for any of us to suffer this casualty of conscience. A very popular song in America during the days of World War II was a little ditty attributed to a chaplain at Pearl Harbor, "Praise the Lord and Pass the Ammunition." In those days it was actually possible for a Christian to think that he could praise God and at the same time kill God's children. How difficult it is sometimes for God to get his word through to us!

We were highly amused at the press notices informing us that the Indians in North Carolina not long ago took to the warpath again. They were endeavoring to break up a Ku Klux Klan rally following the burning of a number of fiery crosses on the lawns of Indian residents who were not desired by their white neighbors. (Perhaps the Indians were a little too American to suit them!) These klansmen were in some cases sincere church members who actually believed that it was in order to use the sign of the cross not for the redemption of all men but for the rejection of some. Thus may our conscience be warped in such a manner that God cannot break into it at all.

Now in the days when David was king it was the right of every citizen to appeal directly to the king for the adjudication of civil or criminal disputes. Israel had its judges before it had its kings. The first king was simply an anointed judge, so the tradition that any citizen could appeal a case of injustice to the king was carried on. David was a just judge and a devout worshiper. When Nathan came to him with a tale of a poor man whose only lamb had been taken taken away from him by a rich man his sense of justice was deeply disturbed, and he decreed that the exploiter should die. David was quick to see the sin of the other man but slow to perceive that Nathan was merely drawing a parable of his own sin.

Insensitivity to our own guilt is commonplace. Many churchmen will kick up a big fuss when supermarkets announce their intention to remain open on Sundays, yet these same churchmen will not hesitate to patronize competing markets on their way home from church and thus to make it difficult for their employees to enjoy Sabbath-day worship and fellowship with their families. An almost sure way for a minister to make himself unpopular with his congregation is to mention that the owners of substandard housing in slum neighborhoods are contributors to juvenile delinquency. I much prefer to hear a sermon that pats me on the back and makes me feel good than to hear one that gives me a swift kick and makes me aware of my own sins.

Somebody had to smuggle God's thoughts into David's hardened heart, so Nathan came to him. Nathan was the one man who had the courage to volunteer for an audience with the king and to speak to him about his sin.

It is never easy to approach someone else critically. We are always fearful lest we hurt the other's feelings. A teenage boy in a church I once served was having a terrible time attracting any interest from the opposite sex. The girls fell for all his friends, but he was never able to get a date. One day he came to see me. He wanted to know why he was not popular with girls. I told him that he was overly aggressive—that he pushed himself so hard that the girls dreaded to see him approaching. He looked at me quietly and said, "Why didn't you tell me this before?" And he was absolutely right! What kind of pastor, what kind of friend, was I to this boy that I would stand by in silence and watch him commit social suicide? Mine was the responsibility to come to him with the truth about himself. It was not he who had failed. I had failed.

Florence Nightingale, the nurse, was called "the Angel of the Crimea." Why? Because she was willing to go to the place where she was needed as God's messenger. We don't need wings to be angels; we need two feet and the willingness to walk with him on his errands!

Perhaps God sent you to the place where you are to be his voice to a mixed-up friend. I am always interested in the reaction of servicemen to their tour of military duty. Some consider it "time out" from living, a fruitless interruption of their life plans. If the primary objective in life is to make money, to become established in an occupation, and to settle down the years in service are indeed a waste of time. If, however, the purpose of life is to make friends, to serve men, and to find one's self, then the years of involuntary service may be rather "time in" for living! There is an abundance of time during the draftee's tour of duty for him to come into close contact with men whose lives are hopelessly adrift and devoid of purpose or target. He may be sent to a lonely outpost in order that he may meet and serve the needs of such a friend. If so, he goes as God's messenger— as an angel without wings. As once he spoke through Nathan so now he speaks again.

Nathan Said to David, "You Are The Man. Thus Says the Lord."

It is a delicate job trying to prick the other fellow's conscience. Note that Nathan did not approach David by denouncing his sin and thereby raising his defenses. Rather he crept up slyly upon him.

A flank attack is often more effective than a frontal assault. Just upstream from the city of Quebec lie the Plains of Abraham on the top of a bluff overlooking the Saint Lawrence River valley. It was there that the British wrested control of Canada away from the French. How? The French held what seemed an impregnable fortress, totally immune to frontal attack. But they did not reckon upon canoes skimming quietly across the water at night and landing their passengers in the reeds along the shoreline, nor did they expect the British to scale the side of the cliff in the darkness of night. It was thus that Wolfe defeated Montcalm.

42

Nathan was smart enough to creep up on the lee side of David. He appealed to this just judge to make a decision in an imaginary case. Appealing to David's sense of justice through the parable he was able to remind the king of God's judgment toward him. Inherent in every man is a certain sense of decency, and an appeal to that sense of decency is far more effective than a blunt condemnation of a man's sin.

I used to work in a bank in Hollywood, and every Monday morning I listened to the fellows describing their weekend exploits with women. One young man was particularly proud of his "record." One weekend, however, he spent with a girl for whom he had developed a genuine affection. He never assaulted her, and when asked why by one of the other fellows, he replied, "Oh, I wouldn't touch her. I love her!" If we can tap this basic good in another person we can become messengers of God far more effectively than if we make them defensive by simply "bawling them out."

Perhaps the reason Alcoholics Anonymous has been more effective than many churchmen in drying up drunks is the fact that an A.A. member approaches an alcoholic not in the note of condemnation, but as a fellow struggler.

A certain football team had played a miserable first half. They went to the dressing room between halves in fear and trepidation. What would the coach say? To their utter amazement he said absolutely nothing! The silence in the dressing room became almost oppressive as half time wore on. Then the buzzer sounded warning the team to return to the field. At this point the coach said, "Well, girls, half time is over!" That was all that was needed. It is not always necessary to scold. More effective than the nagging wife or the scolding teacher is someone who concentrates on drawing out the best in us rather than denouncing our failures.

The carrier waves for God's voice surround us on every side crying, "You are the man!" A little child is building a house out of blocks. On the rear of it he adds a very tiny little room. His father asks, "What is the little room for?" Sonny replies, "For you and mommy to live in when you get old." Then the father remembers the family discussions concerning where to put grandma. The birds come home to roost!

Perhaps the most effective rebukes that come to the American people are not declarations by writers of foreign books of faults in our culture, but are the searching questions frequently asked of the man in the street by the visiting foreigner. An embarrassing question is more pointed than any parable. The Department of State maintains a reception center in Honolulu for the purpose of establishing personal contacts between individual American citizens and incoming visitors of prominence from various Pacific nations. Honolulu residents volunteer to drive these visitors about so that they may see what typical American homes are like and may have the opportunity to visit in those homes where there are children and pets and where life is real and not as depicted by Hollywood films. A distinguished Oriental was one of the visitors. His host was endeavoring to impress upon him the advanced standard of living in our country. "Driving on the freeway I can cut my driving time to the office in half," he said. "By using electronics in my office I can cut my bookkeeping time to one third. The electrical appliances in our home enable my wife to do her housework in half the time. These have been the fruits of American inventiveness and progress." He looked at the visitor to see if he had made an impression.

After a moment of reflection the Oriental asked, "And what do you do with the time that you save?"

Perhaps the most effective rebuke of all is that which comes from standing in the presence of a finer person. Many of us remember the incident in Lloyd C. Douglas' novel *The Robe* following the crucifixion of Jesus. Marcellus, the Roman soldier, had been drinking heavily to escape from the unpleasantness of his assignment of watching Jesus die. After they take the body from the cross and fold the bloody and sweat-stained garments Marcellus, dazed, drunk, and exhausted, returns to his quarters. In a moment of privacy with his servant he mumbles, "I'm dirty. . . . I'm dirty—outside and inside. I'm dirty—and ashamed. Understand, Demetrius? I'm dirty and ashamed." He had seen the contrast between himself and the matchless personality of Jesus. I am reminded of a time in junior high school when I used an expression that was popular but not very refined. My buddy looked at me and said simply, "That isn't like you." I never used that word again. The Lord spoke to David through a stranger and so now he speaks again.

"Then Nathan Went to His House."

Nathan's work was done until he was called back to anoint Solomon king. He did not become a guardian angel over David—this is hard for some well-meaning religious folk to understand. Real angels don't "harp" on something! The word of the Lord is delivered once; it is not a persisting commercial. To be God's messenger to someone else does not mean that we must become that person's permanent and professional conscience. We must discharge our mission and then, like Nathan, go back to minding our own affairs.

Even as the church has both a prophetic and a priestly function, so the individual Christian is called not simply to denounce the sins of others but so to live day by day that others will avoid stumbling. The most effective way to fight against lewdness on the movie screen or in smutty literature is to patronize clean shows and to buy the books that are constructive. Theater owners feel compelled to exhibit the pictures that bring in the best "box office," and publishers will print what the public will read. The best Christian witness is the affirmative witness that is borne in the daily routine of supporting that which is worthy and shunning that which is evil.

In the early days of the temperance movement a woman crusader marched into a saloon and began haranguing the customers to leave such an evil place. The proprietor walked up to her and said, "Madam, I am engaging in a perfectly lawful business. If you do not believe that my business should be allowed why don't you expend your energy at the ballot box instead of trying to intimidate my customers?"

The reformer considered this for a moment, then put out her hand and said, "Shake! You're right!" She then went back to her house, as Nathan did, and began the slower but more effective process of resistance at the points where it counts.

It is always more appealing to engage in a dramatic crusade than to go back to the routine of decent living and the power of simple example. Yet for every man who has been challenged and transformed by the rebuke of a prophet there may be a dozen men whose lives are transformed by the friendship and wholesome example of a dedicated priest or pastor or a Christian layman. Nathan was called one day to a dramatic witness, but he was called for many more days to a quiet witness. The mother in the home or the Christian businessman practicing honesty and exhibiting concern for both his employees and his customers in the long run comprise the host of witnesses who turn men from the ways of darkness to the ways of light. "Let your light so shine" was spoken of a candle—not of a searchlight!

So now he speaks again—in the challenging words and the constructive criticism of a friend. This is the redemptive fellowship of the church. Churchmen do not profess to be angels in the sense of becoming unearthly creatures. If we tear the wings off the angels, however, we find in our fellowship many who have been the messengers of God bringing out the best and the finest within us. And there is no higher calling!

5
all shook up!

Text: Isa. 6:1-8

CRISIS IN THE CONGO HAD TERRIFIED THE WHOLE WORLD. THE
province of Katanga was in revolt, desiring to secede from
the new Congolese nation. The free world feared that Com-
munist intervention in this crisis might trigger a third
world war. If the United Nations "lost face" in this contest
of authority its future capacity for peacemaking seemed
doomed. The hopes and fears of millions rode with Dag
Hammarskjold, secretary general of the United Nations, as
his plane took off for the Congo, where he hoped to effect a
settlement. Then came the tragic news. The quiet, brave
man of all nations had perished as his plane crashed, and
the hopes of men of goodwill everywhere were dashed to
bits with his shattered aircraft. Who could now save the
peace?

It is always so when our security is suddenly taken away
from us. We feel "all shook up" and wonder what is going
to happen to us next. Whether the loss is that of a leader,
a loved one, or a job the reaction is always the same.

So it was that the young composer of dynastic ballads for the court, Isaiah, was "all shook up" "in the year that King Uzziah died." After all, Isaiah owed his appointment as the court composer to this king, and now that his patron was gone his future was in doubt. Even more serious, however, was the loss to the nation of a good king at the very moment when the Assyrian Empire to the north was steadily expanding in Israel's direction. His sense of panic was not unlike that which might well pervade a modern nation surrounded on all sides by Soviet expansion. So he did the thing that many of us are wont to do in our hour of trouble. He went to church! In times of despair people usually seek religious solace, and the upset Isaiah went to the Temple. There God spoke to the overwhelmed man. And so now he speaks again to us.

God Spoke to Isaiah in the Symbols of Worship—And so Now He Speaks Again.

One Sunday one of the members of our youth choir told me that she had peeked at the congregation during the pastoral prayer. It surprised her to see how many of the worshipers did not have their heads bowed, but instead, gazed up steadfastly at the thirty-foot glass cross built into the wall above the altar. It did not surprise me, for all through the week I observe confused people coming into the sanctuary to sit still for awhile and think. The symbols of our faith help to stay their minds on God, and they leave with a sense of exaltation of spirit. They remind me of the peasant who habitually went to the cathedral to pray each day. For a long time he would kneel at the Communion rail

49

before he arose to leave. One day the priest asked him what he did so long before the altar. "Father," replied the peasant, "I just look at God for awhile and he looks at me." That is the heart of the worship experience for anyone!

As Isaiah gazed at the altar the smoke of the sacrifices being offered upon it began to take shape until out of hazy confusion there emerged a pattern and a challenge. Every sacred symbol is a reminder of God, and as Isaiah gazed at the altar it seemed to him that the rising smoke assumed the shape of six-winged seraphim or divine messengers. Call it an optical illusion if you will, but the fact remains that in his contemplation of the historic symbols of his faith Isaiah found the Lord, and when he saw the Lord "high and lifted up" he began to change. For the first time he saw himself and his crowd as they really were—unclean!

Isaiah went to the Temple disturbed about his country, but in the Temple he became disturbed about himself. It is often thus. Did you ever stand at the door of a church on Sunday morning and wonder what impelled the various worshipers to attend? Some may have come primarily to meet their friends. Another churchgoer is worried about a serious problem he faces and has come to pray for an answer. Yet another is seeking to find meaning in life. As the service unfolds, however, these people who came to seek different things are gradually welded into one company. The Scriptures, the music, the liturgy, and the prayers bring successive moods to all—the feeling of being overwhelmed, the sense of guilt and then forgiveness, and a

50

challenge and a reassurance. The symbols have become more than books and notes of music; they have become "the means of grace," the instruments that have amplified the voice of God as he speaks to each person. So now he speaks again to us if we have had a true experience of worship.

God Spoke to Isaiah by Puncturing His Alibis—And so Now He Speaks Again.

The purpose of worship is not to make us feel miserable but to make us feel necessary. The true test of its effectiveness is not simply the degree of guilt and contrition which we experience, but it is also the degree of challenge and response which we experience.

Isaiah couldn't get away with an alibi. His protest, "I am a man of unclean lips, and I dwell in the midst of a people of unclean lips," did not suffice to excuse him from the service of God. In his moment of repentance he imagined that one of the filmy seraphim lifted a glowing coal from the altar and touched it to his lips with tongs. In other words, he sensed that God took the initiative in cleansing him of his guilt providing that he was willing to respond to God's will.

Dr. John Hutton used to talk of a young intellectual who frequented his study for interviews concerning his doubts about religion. If it was not the divinity of Jesus which disturbed him, it was the inspiration of the Scriptures, the miracles, or the Resurrection. For a long time Dr. Hutton listened patiently and tried to help the young man think through his problems, but it began to dawn on him that the youth's real difficulties were not intellectual but spirit-

51

ual. One day when the lad came in for another interview concerning another problem Dr. Hutton looked him in the eye and asked, "Tell me, have you by any chance had difficulties with the Ten Commandments?" It was a frontal attack, and it proved completely effective. God gives the lie to all our alibis, even as he did to Isaiah's.

When farmer Harry Holt of Oregon began his famed task of adopting Korean war orphans and then of placing others by the hundreds in American homes for adoption the story of his work made *Life* magazine. Tom Denman, pastor of First Methodist Church in La Jolla, California, was impressed with the article. He told his wife there ought to be more Christians like Holt in this world.

"Why tell me?" she asked. "Why don't you write Mr. Holt a letter of appreciation?" This Tom Denman did, and then he forgot the matter. Some weeks later, however, while he was in bed with flu his bedside telephone rang, and to his amazement it was Mr. Holt calling him.

"Your letter was so understanding of my feelings about these children," Holt said, "that I am sure you will be sympathetic to my problem. I have some children who need good homes, and I am sure a man with your insights will want to adopt some of them."

"*Some* of them?" This was a startling thought to Tom Denman! He began to protest. "But I have a family of three children already. I am living on a Methodist minister's salary. I would love to help but. . . ."

Some months later I saw Tom Denman as he passed through Honolulu on his way to Korea to pick up three children, and last Christmas I received a photo-card of his six children—three Caucasian and three Korean! Tom Denman had thought and prayed about this problem and had come to realize what God could do through him and with him. He undertook the impossible and found it possible because he had looked at God long enough to sense his personal responsibility.

God Spoke to Isaiah as He Began to Realize His Own Possibilities—And so Now He Speaks Again.

The longer Isaiah looked at God the more he realized what God could do for him and with him. Do you remember the life of George Washington Carver, the Negro who came out of a background of slavery to rank as one of America's foremost scientists? Carver told how he was anxious to make some great scientific discovery, but how the vast field of science overwhelmed him in trying to find a toehold. Finally, after much prayer, God seemed to cut him down to size, and he felt that his calling was to begin conducting research on the lowly peanut! This was a staple crop among many of the impoverished tenant farmers of the South, and Dr. Carver realized that if he could discover any additional uses for the peanut or its by-products he could contribute much toward raising the living standards of his poverty-stricken people. Once he began working in this field God opened before him discoveries that have lifted him to the heights of scientific achievement. It is amazing what God can do with what we have to offer.

When you are "all shook up" have you ever considered the divine resources at hand? A bridge was to be removed from across an inland waterway in eastern North Carolina.

It appeared to be a stupendous operation. Yet engineers simply floated two barges under the bridge at low tide and wedged them tightly. Within a very few hours the tide had come in and the bridge was lifted clear. It was then a simple matter to float the bridge downstream and to set it down on new pilings prepared in advance. Have you checked the resources that are at hand to solve your problems?

A few years ago Admiral Richard E. Byrd spent long lonely months in the frozen solitude of the Antartic. There he made a personal discovery as important as any he ever made in his geographical explorations. After he got home he described it in these words: "Few men during their lifetime come anywhere near exhausting the resources dwelling within them. There are deep wells of strength that are never used." Have you not seen these wells tapped by physically handicapped persons—by those who are blind, by those who are deaf, by those who are chronic invalids?

God may have removed the one you depended upon, but he didn't remove you from the scene, and what is to stop you from moving into the King's Row? John Van Ess played on the football team next to a magnificent physical speciman named Harry Wiersum. He was three years Van Ess's senior and was headed for missionary work among the Arabs. Day and night he talked of nothing else. After graduation he took his seminary course and went out to Arabia. At the end of a brief year he succumbed to smallpox, and the call came for someone to take his place. John Van Ess said, "It was as if the signal came to me from the great Captain to carry the ball. For more than forty years now

I have been struggling toward the goal, but never with one regret."

"Here I am. Send me" is the only sound response to tragedy.

God Spoke to the Overwhelmed Isaiah in the Empowering Experience of the Holy Spirit—And so Now He Speaks Again.

Isaiah had entered the Temple in worry and despair because he could find no human spirit adequate for the nation's leadership in an hour of crisis. He left the Temple empowered by the discovery that we aren't left to our own devices. God is our prompter, and his Holy Spirit can work through us if we sincerely confess our own inadequacy and ask for his guidance. He is equal to any emergency. We need only to be big enough to admit our weakness and to accept his will in lieu of our own.

When William Gladstone was prime minister of the British Empire he bore heavy burdens of state. Sometimes he would disappear for a day or two, and those who knew him realized that he had gone off to "seek that help which comes from taking the Sacrament, from reading of the Bible, and from the exercise of prayer." His lifelong habits of Christian trust and devotion upheld him.

On the American scene we find the act of worship giving similar power to President Lincoln. One day in a hospital just after the crucial battle of Gettysburg a General asked him if he wasn't afraid during the battle.

"No!" answered Lincoln. "I was afraid for awhile, General, but I soon got over that. Everybody about me was afraid, and they wanted us to move the government away from Washington, but I knew it would be all right." "Why were you not afraid?" asked the General.

Lincoln was silent for a moment and then replied, "Why, General, I went to my room and got down on my knees and prayed that God would save the Republic. I asked God to give me Gettysburg. I asked God to save Gettysburg for the nation. I asked him to give me Gettysburg, and, General, God said to me, 'I will give you Gettysburg, Abraham, don't worry about it. Just trust in me. I will give you Gettysburg, and freedom for generations yet to be!"

As to Isaiah and to Gladstone and to Lincoln so now he speaks again to us in the empowering experience of worship. Archbishop Trench put it this way:

> Lord, what a change within us one short hour
> Spent in Thy presence will prevail to make!
> What heavy burdens from our bosoms take,
> What parched grounds refresh as with a
>   shower!
> We kneel, and all around us seems to lower;
> We rise, and all, the distant and the near,
> Stands forth in sunny outline brave and clear;
> We kneel how weak! we rise, how full of
>   power!
>
> Why, therefore, should we do ourselves this
>   wrong,
> Or others, that we are not always strong,

That we are ever overborne with care,
That we should ever weak or heartless be,
Anxious or troubled, when with us is prayer,
And joy and strength and courage are with
Thee!

All Shook Up?

'That we are ever overborne with care,
That we should ever wish or ask for less,
Amaze or trouble, when with us is peace,
And joy and strength and courage are with
Thee'

6
he did it with mirrors

Text: Amos 1:1; 4:1-3; 5:21-24; 6:1, 4-8; 7:10-17

STEPHEN VINCENT BENÉT, IN HIS POEM "JOHN BROWN'S Body," tells of a sea captain in the African slave traffic who was pious and prayed regularly but saw nothing wrong about his business. Tradition has it that Sir John Bowring, when he was governor general of Hong Kong, encouraged the opium trade with China. Yet Sir John wrote the tenderly beautiful hymn "In the Cross of Christ I glory." Many of us might be tempted to call him a hypocrite, but his hypocrisy was not much different from our own, for we all suffer from spiritual blindness.

That is God's greatest problem: How to speak to "those who are at ease in Zion." It bothered him at the gigantic religious "barbecue" which the members of "First Church, Samaria" were conducting at the historic shrine at Bethel. Here was a great company of prosperous and complacent Israelites assembled at their place of worship to engage in a ceremony of sacrifice and honor to their God, yet totally oblivious to the ways in which they had prospered by the exploitation of labor and the extortion of the poor. Such complacency is characteristic of periods of prosperity, and the problem which God always faces in such a time of self-satisfaction is how to get his word through to the people. On this particular occasion he found a voice in a country boy who came into the city to see a religious festival. Amos was a poor herdsman who had to supplement his income by tree surgery on the sycamore trees, which bore an insipid figlike fruit that was often filled with insects, so was consumed only by the poor. Unaccustomed as he was to the class distinctions and the complacency of the city, he was horrified to behold the poverty of the masses while their religious leaders lived so extravagantly. This "local yokel" dared to open his mouth as a prophet and speak to the complacent and overfed revelers in the name of God.

How did God finally speak to a period of prosperity? He did it with mirrors! He turned the people's gaze first toward the sins of their neighboring states and thereby gained their attention. You can always get an audience when you talk about the woman down the street! Crowds will always gather to hear what they want to hear. Anybody can get a crowd by announcing that he is going to "expose" someone or something. Amos got his crowd by starting an "anti" crusade, but then God turned the mirror mercilessly upon the Israelites themselves and revealed to them the crassness of their own materialism. And so now he speaks again to us in our prosperous time.

God Had to Resort to Shock Treatment for Israel—And so Now He Speaks Again.

Nations are very much like our human bodies; they do not fail in their construction; they just deteriorate in use. The body of an old person has the same equipment for breathing and digesting and muscular action which is found in the body of a youth, but because many of these organs have been overworked or misused they no longer function. In like manner, a nation may preserve its constitution and its cultural heritage but begin to deteriorate because of lack of care for the maintenance of its talents. If we call the roll of the vanished empires we will appreciate how one by one they deteriorated morally in a period of maximum prosperity. Rome fell at the height of her prosperity, so did the Spanish empire, so did the French empire. The most perilous time in which to live is the period of economic prosperity and moral poverty.

I am reminded of the parable in which Soren Kierkegaard, the Danish philosopher and theologian, likens the Christians of his day to a flock of geese living in a barnyard. Every seventh day they paraded to a corner of the yard, and their most eloquent orator got up on the fence and spoke on the glorious destiny of geese. He spoke of the mercy of the Creator, who had given geese wings and the instinct to fly. He told how they were to use their wings to fly away, for they were only pilgrims on earth. This deeply impressed the geese, who nodded their heads solemnly. They applauded the eloquence of the preaching goose. All this they did, but one thing they did not do.

They did not fly, for the corn was good and the barnyard secure.

This is the peril of prosperity—that we shall develop a false sense of security in the things that we possess rather than in the kind of persons that we are. Do you not know persons who have equated the kingdom of God with the American way of life—and then have equated the American way with their own way? Opposition to Communism may be born of a sincere ideological cleavage, or it may be born of nothing nobler than fear of the loss of privileges!

Only one method seems adequate to rouse "those who are at ease in Zion" out of their lethargy, and that is the method of complete shock. God had to speak in shocking terms to comfortable Samaria, and so now he speaks again to complacent America. It took the successful launching of a satellite by the Russians to make us give any consideration to the possibility that we were not the most secure and brilliant nation upon the earth. When God wanted to arouse America from its all-time high in prosperity and corresponding low in morality he did it with mirrors— exposing our weaknesses. Now we have begun to examine our educational system seriously. Now we begin to be disturbed by the mounting tide of juvenile delinquency. Now we begin to realize that being the richest nation on earth is not synonymous with being the strongest.

André Maurois quotes an Episcopal minister in *A Journal From Missouri*. "Oh, to be sure, our country is well heated, well fed, and the most self-sufficient in the world. We bring up, in comfortable colleges, comfortable children who, after a comfortable marriage, will build a comfortable home where they will wait the moment for going, in a comfortable coffin, to a comfortable grave. But is this the way to save the world?" The Romans built aqueducts and vast road systems and splendid buildings; they financed the greatest war machine on earth; but their plumbing, their engineering, and their military machine did not save them from moral obsolescence.

God Spoke to the "Well-Fixed" Through the Insecure— And so Now He Speaks Again.

Amos' language was crude but vivid. He looked at the overfed Israelite women before him and brazenly addressed them by shouting, "You cows of Bashan." Making such a remark about the woman's society was hardly the way to get off to a diplomatic start with the members of the Samaritan synagogue. Yet this unpolished yokel saw the exploitation of the poor and held up a highly polished mirror to reveal the sins of the self-satisfied. Sometimes it takes an outsider to detect the faults of the insiders.

Some years ago a man was chosen by the American Railway Express Company to negotiate all their labor disputes. They did not choose a school-of-business-administration graduate for this delicate task. They chose a man who had risen from the ranks and who knew what it was to drive an express wagon. There is no substitute for the insight of one who has known insecurity.

Are you listening for the voice of God from the wrong quarter? It comes from below as often as from above!

Future historians may well record the name of a Negro student of our generation, Autherine Lucy. She may be the one who marked the turning point in the national conscience toward racial integration in our schools, for it was the efforts of this previously unknown girl to enroll in a school for which she was academically qualified that focused the eyes of the nation on the injustice to the American Negro. It was a little old man wrapped in a white sheet sitting before a spinning wheel who brought independence to the untouchables of India and who brought liberty to the millions of that land. We might expect to look to the pulpit or to the college faculty for leadership, but God does not always speak from the expected sources. Leadership does not always come down from above. Sometimes it rises from below.

Jesus said that the meek shall inherit the earth. Haven't they already? The militarists who swept across Japan assassinating all the liberals have disappeared from human history in just a few years, but the unarmed Japanese peasant is still with us, and the defeated nation that was stripped of her arms has regained ascendancy in the Orient. So now he speaks again in a mighty chorus of voices from the disinherited of the earth. We would do well to listen to the cries for freedom of the dark-skinned millions of the earth who seethe with revolt and the desire for recognition in these times. Woe to us if we are "at ease in Zion" and permit our material prosperity in the American way of life to blind us to the spiritual values that constitute the only solid foundation for national survival.

God Pricked the Conscience of Samaritan Churchmen with "Rear-Vision Mirrors"—And so Now He Speaks Again.

Amos showed the would-be worshipers the world of misery at their door. Until he came they had been blind to it. Those who have visited in the Far East have surely noticed that the Buddhist and Shinto shrines in those lands become the centers for crowds of beggars and the most wretched of the poor. It never seems to occur to the devout as they make their way to the shrines to kneel in isolated adoration of their ancestors that their contemporaries who throng the temple courtyard deserve the attention of those who are truly religious. Their minds are so stayed upon their individual religious experiences that they have no sense of relationship to the social scene about them. Among their Christian brethren are likewise those who are so intoxicated with the joy of their individual salvation that they find no time for concern about the helpless victims of "man's inhumanity to man."

The late Ernest Fremont Tittle used to speak of "convenient ignorance." "If I do not know too much about the misery of others," he said, "I may not feel called upon to do anything about it." It is so very easy to dismiss the miserable from our doorstep by simply paying no attention to them. I am reminded of two men traveling together on a train through the slum area of one of our industrial cities. One of the men pulled down the shade and remarked, "It always depresses me to see so much poverty and not be able to do anything about it."

"But there is something you can do about it," replied his seatmate. "You can pull up the shade!"

When I was at Garrett Biblical Institute in Evanston, Illinois, I went to visit an aunt of mine who lived in Chicago. She asked if there was anything I especially wanted to see in that great city. I replied that there was; I wanted to visit Maxwell Street down in the ghetto.

"Why do you want to see such a depressing neighborhood as that?" she asked. "We have libraries, art galleries, museums, concerts—so much that is beautiful and happy in Chicago, and you want to see an awful place like that!" She wanted me to shut my eyes to the evil side of life and see only the good side.

We are born with two eyes, however—one to see the nobility in every person and the beauty and joy in everyday life, and the other to be aware of the evil in men and of the misery that stalks on every hand. To go through life with either eye closed is only to half live. Yet there are many who want to go through life in exactly that way.

One such was Amaziah, the high priest. He tried to get rid of Amos. He told him to go away, that he was disturbing the people. Amaziah could not escape the consequences of truth, however. Recently I heard of a man who said, "I am so disturbed by all this talk about cigarettes and cancer that I have decided to give up reading about it!" "Please go away and let me sleep" may be an easy attitude, but it will not alter the facts. God had to speak of unpleasant things through Amos—and so now he speaks again to our own times.

He is speaking through the "blackboard jungle" that is

overgrowing our cities. He is speaking through the refugees that every day wriggle through the Iron Sieve in quest of freedom. The facts of life are as discomforting today as they were in the days of Amos. Only those who see them laid bare will be stirred to clamber down out of the lap of luxury and get into the struggle for justice and peace on earth.

There is a sign on a dairy back in Colorado which reads "Our cows are not contented; they are striving to do better!" How about you?

7
rubble raisers or
rabble rousers?

Text: Neh. 1:1-4, 11b; 2:1-6, 11-12, 15-18

WHEREVER WE GO IN THIS POSTWAR WORLD WE MEET DIS-
placed persons. The cashier at one of Honolulu's most
popular restaurants was secretary to the German scientist
Albert Einstein before the war forced his exile in America.
We have been reading in periodicals of late how the scientists who developed the successful rockets which launched
our American satellites were themselves German scientists
displaced to this country by the war. Never a week goes
by in Honolulu that does not see distinguished visitors passing through that port who have been displaced from their
former homeland by the forces of evil. This is no modern
phenomenon, however. It was true of the Jews in many periods in history, and especially so at the period of the Baby-
lonian exile.

The Babylonians were very smart in their conquest of
the Jews. They did not try to deport the common laborers;

they took the intellectuals and the leaders of the people away into Babylon, knowing full well that a leaderless people would never arise to any accomplishments. It is in this situation that we meet a contractor named Nehemiah who was assigned to be the king's bartender—or cupbearer if you prefer. God spoke to Nehemiah out of the rubble of frustration and so now he speaks again to us.

God Spoke to Nehemiah's Sleeping Genius Through the Reports of Travelers—And so Now He Speaks Again.

Nehemiah was an experienced builder and engineer, but with the characteristic policy of the military he was not assigned to this field of his maximum experience but, instead, was assigned to the menial task of domestic winebearer to the king. The job hardly became him, but nevertheless the softness of court life in the capital city of Susa overpowered Nehemiah until he began to lose interest in the building trade and to become almost content with the easy but demoralizing life of the palace.

Prosperity can win us away from our natural bents. The lure of a well-paying job can sidetrack us from the pursuit of an education or a vocation for which we are naturally endowed and can result in a tragic exchange of capacity for comfort. Sleeping genius needs only a shock to awaken it, however, and God gave a rude awakening to Nehemiah in a way that sounds quite familiar to many of us.

Hanani, one of his kinsmen, returned from a trip to Jerusalem in the company of several travelers who bore disturbing reports. They told Nehemiah of the demoralization of his hometown. They told how the walls of Jerusalem were in ruins and how the leaderless people were stupidly resigned to the humiliation which they had suffered at the hands of the Babylonians. This shocked Nehemiah, for to the Jew of that time Jerusalem was far more than a former capital city—it was a sacred shrine. Since the collapse of their state the Jews had nothing but their religion left to bind them together as a people, and the Temple at Jerusalem, which had long been the headquarters of that religion, must not be desecrated or the last vestige of their ethnic bonds would be broken. Nehemiah wept long and prayed much concerning the demoralization that had overtaken his people.

It was not the only time that the reports of travelers have aroused the conscience of men. Few of us remember the name of J. K. Studd, but nearly all of us recognize the name of the great John R. Mott who founded the international Y.M.C.A. and laid the first foundations for the interfaith ecumenical movement of today. Yet this probably would not have been the career of John R. Mott had not Dr. Studd visited the campus of Cornell University while Mott was a sophomore. In a chapel address and in a subsequent interview with the young sophomore, Dr. Studd challenged him with the need for a broader point of view, and the disturbing reports from this world traveler awakened Mott's sleeping genius.

At the quadrennial conference of the Methodist Student Movement at Kansas University Roy Sasaki, a young Japanese-American from Hawaii, sat in the audience. Three years later I talked with Roy at Garrett Biblical Institute and expressed the hope that this dynamic native of Hawaii would return to the Islands to work in the mission. At first I was disappointed to hear him say that he never intended to return to Hawaii, but I understood when he told me why. One of the speakers at the quadrennial student gathering was Bishop Newell Booth of Africa. "After listening to the tragic needs of the African people as stated by Dr. Booth," said Roy, "I could never live with myself if I do not volunteer to go as a missionary to Africa." Another traveler with a disturbing report had awakened the genius of another potential Christian leader.

Sir Wilfred Grenfell, the great English missionary physician who devoted his life to improving the living conditions of the inhabitants of Labrador and Newfoundland, often went to college student bodies for recruits. "We have to determine," he would say to the students, "whether this world is an arena where we fight to get what we can for ourselves, or a field of honor where we give all we can for our fellow men." Following his appeal young men would spring to their feet by the score as volunteers to go with him to wrestle with cold, ignorance, and disease.

The best missionary cultivation is done by returning travelers. A retired traveler, Dr. Glenn Flynn, made a trip to Hawaii several years ago and sensed the tremendous opportunity there in the field of student work. With his experience in student work he readily sensed the challenge of the "mission field within a mission field" presented by the university campus, where forty per cent of the 8,500 students come from Buddhist homes. He went back to Texas, told the story of what he had seen, and was able to raise thirty thousand dollars there toward the erection of an adequate new building for the university Wesley Foundation. The Division of National Missions and the First Methodist Church of Palo Alto, California, brought the total up to eighty thousand dollars. Such is the type of missionary work that can be done by a returning traveler. It is for this reason that the Methodist Men of First Methodist Church, Honolulu, never tire of volunteering their services to show visitors the work of their missionary dollars in Hawaii. These plain laymen can go home and stir up a wave of missionary enthusiasm surpassing anything that can be produced by pamphlets or visual aids. God spoke to Nehemiah through Hanani and the travelers, and so now he speaks again.

God Spoke to Nehemiah Also Through the Open Doors of Opportunity—And so Now He Speaks Again.

After much prayer and wrestling with what could be done about this disturbing news, Nehemiah suddenly realized his own strategic position in solving the problem. He had prayed much when the thought dramatically occurred to him: "Now I was cupbearer to the king!" If anything was ever going to be done to rebuild both the walls and the morale of Jerusalem it would have to be done by an emissary with royal credentials. What other Jew combined the construction know-how with the inside track to the king's ear and favor which Nehemiah enjoyed? Was he not the king's personal attendant? Was he not in his presence when the king was in the best mood? Before him was an open door of opportunity for service, and through this open door he heard the voice of God. After much prayer for strength and guidance he approached the king and asked for a leave to go to rebuild the walls of Jerusalem. His request was granted.

There is no substitute for the man who is *there*—in a strategic place. Nobody else has the inside track to the ear of a buddy except the friend who sleeps in the rack next to him. Who else sees him sitting on the bunk staring vacantly at the floor when other fellows get mail and he does not? Who else sees the flash of anger as he writes a note, crumples it up, and throws it over the side? Who else knows well as you do the heartbreak of the girl who pounds the typewriter next to yours? Who can speak a cheering word at as strategic a time to the disconsolate customer but the groceryman who chats with him across the counter every day? The front line of evangelism is held by the ranks of the everyday friends of persons who are carrying crushing loads. No inspiring book and no comforting sermon can be as sure of getting to the person in need as you can be sure of establishing contact with a burdened friend. There is no substitute for the man who is there.

I am also a bit nettled when, in the course of a visitation evangelism campaign, a prospect card comes back with the notation by the lay visitor, "I was unable to secure a decision from this person, but believe that if the pastor would call he might do so." If you cannot sell the Christian faith by the contagion of your own spirit it will never be sold by the theological knowledge of a professional religionist. Religion is caught; it is not taught. The man who has the opportunity to visit with a person in his hour of extremity can do a far more effective evangelistic task than any preacher can do in his pulpit on Sunday morning. There is no substitute for the man who is there.

A businessman told me one Christmastime that he had had to attend half a dozen office parties during that week. "I don't enjoy going to those affairs," he said, "but if I can show those folks that it is possible to have a good time without drinking liquor then I feel I can render a witness in that circle that could not be rendered by anyone else." There is no substitute for the man who is there. There was none for Nehemiah, and there is none for us. God speaks again through the open doorway of daily opportunities for witness.

God Spoke When Nehemiah Searched for the Truth— And so Now He Speaks Again.

"Then I went up in the night . . . and inspected the wall," wrote Nehemiah. God expects us to ascertain the facts for ourselves before we rush in hastily to foolish action.

I was enormously proud of our Woman's Division of Christian Service in Honolulu. For many years they operated an excellent boarding home there for children from broken or delinquent homes—the Susannah Wesley Home. Then came a change in the policy of the social agencies. They realize now that no institution however fine can be an equal substitute for a Christian home and normal contacts with a mother and a father. Needy children are now placed in foster homes, and there are no more referrals to Susannah Wesley. What should the women do? For a time they tried to meet the expressed need for a rehabilitation center for emotionally disturbed children, but they soon discovered that the psychiatric staff required by such an institution was beyond the limits of their resources to provide. They waited until they had ascertained all the facts of the social needs of the community and then announced that Susannah Wesley would reopen as a desperately needed community center in the Kalihi district. In other words, they went out "in the night . . . and inspected the wall."

The facts are there for us to see if we will take the time to look carefully. Dr. Giles T. Brown of Orange Coast College quotes a survey by the International Press Institute which showed that the average newspaper reader in America spends eighteen minutes a day on this task, only two minutes of which are devoted to the reading of news on foreign affairs. Two minutes a day is not enough for citizens of a self-governing democracy in a position of world leadership in an hour of desperate danger! We are unworthy to lead the world if we are too lazy to acquaint ourselves with the facts about other nations and our relationships with them. The doorways of opportunity are open for us to hear the voice of God, but we have to stand in the doorway long enough to hear his voice. Once he spoke to Nehemiah, and so now he speaks again to us.

God Spoke to Nehemiah Through a Call to Action—And so Now He Speaks Again.

After he had surveyed the ruined walls and noted the sagging morale of the people, and after he had ordered the necessary lumber for its reconstruction, then, and not before, Nehemiah called the people together. "You see the trouble we are in. . . . Come, let us build," he said to them.

74

The time was ripe to persuade the people to stop crying and complaining and to begin working and rebuilding.

A convict had been condemned to hang. He was told that nothing could save him but the governor. Long and painfully he sat in his cell struggling to find words that would explain his predicament. The next morning the governor got this message: "Dear Guvner: They are fixin' to hang me Friday, and here it is Tuesday!" They are fixing to hang our world in the not too distant future, and time is getting away from us. A-bombs, H-bombs, C-bombs, guided missiles, satellites—all these are reminders to us that it is time to stop talking and begin doing something. "You see the trouble we are in. . . . Come, let us build!"

Letters to your Congressmen can accomplish more than you think. Senator Paul H. Douglas of Illinois received a letter from an unknown man protesting that too high a price was being paid for military housing in his area. The senator looked into the situation, found it to be so, and introduced legislation based on the letter which ultimately saved the taxpayers thirty million dollars.

This is the difference between the rubble raiser and the rabbler rouser. Nehemiah didn't make speeches—he made gateways. Our Scout and "Y" leaders, Sunday-school teachers and youth counselors do not wring their hands over juvenile delinquency. They busy themselves providing gateways through which youth can pass into constructive living. They see the trouble we are in and get busy building. They pass milestones instead of resolutions!

In these days when the "apostles of discord" are moving across America sowing seeds of suspicion and distrust of our public officials, our clergymen, and our educators, we need to recognize the distinction between rabble rousers and rubble raisers. It is one thing to wave the flag and denounce Communism, as can be easily done by firing up public emotions. It is a far more effective thing, however, to work away quietly at the task of feeding the hungry, clothing the naked, educating the illiterate, and healing the sick. Some folks are attracting great attention by making fiery anti-Communist speeches, and there is no doubt that people need to be alerted to the menace of Communism. An equally sincere and much larger group, however, is working every day in quieter ways to destroy the evil social conditions upon which Communism feeds and to educate and motivate persons to Christian standards. Long after the rabble rousers have been forgotten, the rubble raisers will leave their lasting monument in schools, hospitals, prosperous agricultural centers, and dedicated public servants.

Action is stronger than propaganda, as the Reds will some day know. God's voice comes to the defeated as a call to action, and if you and I are to be his spokesmen to the frantic age in which we live we must busy ourselves about the task of educating the illiterate, feeding the hungry, and setting disciplined objectives before the bewildered and the confused. We must make their trouble our business.

The slums of Chicago are still far from redeemed, but they would be infinitely worse had not a girl named Jane Addams said in 1889, "Here, this is my affair!" She made their trouble her business, and Hull House stands today as a white spot in a blighted area because of her active concern. The treatment of women in our prisons is not yet perfect, but such advances as have been made began 150 years ago with a Christian named Elizabeth Fry who dared social ostracism to attack the unspeakable conditions in British prisons and to say of them, "Here, this is my affair!" The beautiful billboard-free highways in Hawaii are there to enjoy because a group of public spirited women in the Outdoor Circle said, "Here, this is my affair!"

Are we "living it up" in Susa, or are we working in Jerusalem? We can be noisy rabble rousers, fuming and complaining and stirring up dissension, or we can be constructive rubble raisers, lifting the defeated one brick at a time. "You see the trouble that we are in. . . . Come, let us build!"

8

picking up the pieces of a broken home

Text: Hos. 1:2-4, 6, 8; 2:1-7; 3:2-5

A WOMAN WALKED INTO A PUBLIC LIBRARY AND ASKED THE librarian, "Do you have any books on marriage problems? I married one!"

Socrates said, "Marry by all means. If you get a good wife, you will be very happy. If you get a bad one, you will become a philosopher." John Wesley would probably agree with him! The one chapter in the life of the founder of Methodism which is rarely discussed is his unhappy marriage. Undoubtedly Wesley, with his rigid self-disciplines and his rugged schedule, was a difficult person with whom to live. It also appears that his wife was a bit of a shrew, for after she left him John Wesley recorded in his journal, "I will not divorce her. I shall not pursue her."

On the other hand, the celibate misses a whole world of creative experience. I could never understand the viewpoint of those who feel that their spiritual life will be deepened by denying themselves the exigencies of married life, for certainly if there is any place where love has to learn to be unselfish and where patience is grown, that place is within the relationship of marriage.

No other relationship so closely yokes together those from divergent backgrounds as does marriage. The parent-child and the sibling relationship is forged between those with a mutual background of experience. This is not true of marriage. Love may draw together those of entirely different background. Hence there are many adjustments required in marriage which may lead to friction or may lead to growth.

This brings us to consideration of the heartbroken person who is picking up the pieces of a broken home. Does God have any word for that unhappy multitude of the separated and the divorced? If our gospel is to be good news to all men then it must have a message to those who have found their romance foundering.

God spoke in such a marital misadventure to Hosea, who married a faithless wife, and so now he speaks again to those who are picking up the pieces of a broken home.

God Spoke to Hosea Through the Experience of Estrangement—And so Now He Speaks Again.

It is easy to misunderstand the voice of God. Hosea actually believed that God wanted him to marry a harlot! Indeed, I know of no more startling passage in the Scriptures than that opening statement in the writings of this prophet when God said to him, "Go, take to yourself a wife of harlotry." It is surely inconceivable that a righteous

God would ask a man to marry a woman who is a bad marital risk just in order to make his shattered romance a parable of man's faithlessness to God. Yet Hosea actually fell so much in love with Gomer that he believed his marriage to her was the will of God. If "marriages are made in heaven" as so many persons claim, how does it happen that marriage is hell for so many people?

We have to realize how easy it is to be fooled at first sight. We become very defensive when another person questions the wisdom of our blossoming romance, and we firmly believe that this affair of the heart is the gift of God himself. Usually, however, this is because we do not allow a sufficient time to take a second look.

Mike Connelly, a Hollywood reporter, was interviewing John Barrymore, the actor. Barrymore burst forth with, "Love is the delightful interval between meeting a beautiful girl and discovering she looks like a haddock!" Is this because love is blind? Or is it sex that is blind?

Physical attraction does not wear very well. The time will come when he will bulge in the wrong places and she will sag in the wrong places. The romance that is founded upon nothing but sexual attraction is so strong that it may overpower us completely and paralyze our good judgment. "I never *felt* this way about any other person," you may say, but notice that you are describing a feeling, a sensation, and not a mature judgment. Hosea mistook another voice for God's when he courted Gomer. He listened much more to the siren call of sex than to the qualities of character and spiritual depth which are essential for an enduring marriage.

Therefore his marriage was doomed to failure before it was consummated. Yet he blamed God!

By their estrangement God spoke his rebuke to Hosea for his folly. We can repair but we cannot reinforce a cracked relationship. The weakness is there, and it cannot take much strain! This is true of the pyschology of infidelity. A man may say that he can be promiscuous without his wife's ever knowing it, but the fact remains that when that man comes to search for a way to express the fullness of his love and devotion to his companion of the years he has nothing to offer her but a dark gallery of unwanted images in his memory, which he tries to suppress and merely locks into his subconscious. Psychologists tell us that we never really forget something. If we repress a memory it will arise to haunt us in our dreams or in the form of a twist in our personality. The sexual relationship that has once been cracked by infidelity will crack again under tension, for the consequences of bad memories and unconfessed sins are even more damaging than the consequences of venereal disease.

In like manner, once the crack of jealousy has opened up in a marriage the relationship will always weaken under strain at that point. False accusations will come whenever the pressure builds up, for this is God's continuing rebuke to us for the sin of yielding to jealousy in the first place.

A sound bit of advice to maidens is, "Don't marry a man to reform him. The rites never right him and the altar won't alter him."

Even in love there must be a note of judgment. Hosea saw his children suffer because of his unwise marriage. It is easy for us to call God a monster for bringing suffering upon the innocent children of folly. But how else, in a world of free will, can men ever see the difference between right and wrong? The truth that Hosea perceived, that his children would suffer because of the unwise union which he had made, was but a foretaste of the sociologists' discoveries of our time. Dr. Edgar Lowther of San Francisco, talking with the chaplain at San Quentin penitentiary in California, asked why these men landed in prison. Hastily the chaplain pulled a number of cards from his file and read the case records. The vast majority of cards selected showed broken homes as the cause of the trouble. Truly the sins of the fathers are visited upon the children. You cannot escape the consequences of unwise choices. It is through these consequences that God speaks again to us, as he did to Hosea of the importance of meeting the right kind of prospective companions in the right kind of places and under mature conditions of judgment.

God Spoke to Hosea Through the Experience of Redemptive Love—And so Now He Speaks Again.

Hosea discovered that his love for Gomer persisted even though she spurned him. When she left him and went off after other lovers he found that he did not hate her but continued to love her, however little she deserved or returned his love. Finally he located her in the slave market, and he brought her back—not so much by the merchandise that he traded for her as by the forgiving love which he extended to her. No wonder she said, "I will go and return to my first husband," for none of her subsequent lovers had offered her this kind of suffering love.

Then it was that Hosea realized that this was a parable of God's love for faithless Israel. He began to see that the Covenant relationship between God and the Israelites had been broken by their faithlessness to him and their pursuit of other loves. None of these other loves, however, sustained across the years a forgiving attitude and a continuing concern for the backsliding Jew. The undeserved love of God is the force which draws his children back to him, even as the undeserved love of Hosea brought the faithless Gomer back to him.

Picking up the pieces of a broken home Hosea found a shatterproof love. A channel had been carved in his life for a self-giving love, and though that channel may have drained dry it was still there as a capacity for the conveying of a finer love in later years.

Those who have crossed the desert regions of the Southwest have seen the dry arroyos, or washes, down which the spring freshets rage in muddy torrents on occasion. Most of the year those sandy watercourses are dry and filled with sagebrush. One who does not know the ways of the desert would never believe that they can flow with water, but when the rains descend heavily in the mountains the watercourse once carved out will again become a channel for the life-giving waters into the wastelands.

So it is with the person who has learned how to love. His love may not be returned by the one he loves, but the capacity he has developed for loving and for self-sacrifice will bring to him in time an even richer love. I knew a man who sobbed that his heart was forever broken when his wife deserted him in favor of another man, but so deeply ingrained was this good man's capacity for love for her, even though she neither deserved nor returned it, that in later years a finer woman found that man and gave him a measure of happiness that he had never known before and could never have known without this capacity for loving.

It is quite true that the church does not look with favor upon divorce. At least we do not favor entering into the marriage relationship casually in the thought that it can be quickly terminated if it does not work out happily. On the other hand, it is inconsistent with the teachings and life example of Jesus to contend that the institution of marriage is more important than the personalities of the individuals who are married. Jesus stressed that man is more important than the institution of the Sabbath and that service to man is more important than the preservation of the rituals of the synagogue. Does it seem conceivable then that he would expect mismated individuals to go through life making themselves, their children, and all about them miserable? The injunction against divorce is not a life sentence to keep people permanently unhappy. Rather, it is a forceful reminder to make the right choice in the first place. Is there any one of us as earthly parents who would go on indefinitely punishing a child for a mistake he once made? Is God more unkind than man? It is not the will of God that men should live in permanent misery, but it is his will that men should learn how to love. Once that capacity for love has been developed it will find an outlet somewhere, somehow, someday.

In an Easter hymn we sing "Love's redeeming work is done." But it took awhile to accomplish! It took a long time for the redemptive quality of Hosea's love to bring Gomer back to him, and we must not rush the process of redemption. We can say with certainty, however, that the one who has learned to love redemptively will ultimately inspire a change in the life of even the most indifferent and ungrateful. It may take years before your domestic suffering will seem to make any difference in another's life, but so long as you embody the godlike quality of love you will be his agent in the spiritual redemption of others.

God Spoke to Hosea Through the Experience of a New Relationship Forged in the Heat of Tragedy—And so Now He Speaks Again.

Out of the emptiness of Hosea's life came a companionship—an awareness of the manner in which the love of God paralleled his own. When a man has turned in the love of a maid for the eternal love of God he has not been shortchanged.

God speaks through the heart as well as though the mind. Out of the ruins of his home Hosea built a faith—a faith that was the first in Old Testament theology to perceive God as a lover as well as a judge. When this faith is awakened within us we can endure all manner of pain.

An old Negro woman lived alone in a rude cabin in the hills of Virginia. All her family had died yet she never felt herself to be alone. One day a friendly traveler passed by and called out to ask who lived there. "Nobody but me and Jesus," came the cheery reply. In her loneliness she had found the Great Companion.

I recall chatting with a German lad about his experience during the Allied bombings of his hometown during World War II. "Before that houses and things were important to us," he said. "But when our homes were destroyed and our possessions gone, and many of our loved ones gone too, we realized that the only item remaining to us was our faith. Nobody could bomb God out of our lives, and strengthened by this new discovery of the meaning of his presence, we were able to start life over again."

There is a wonderful symbol of this inward working to be found in the rehabilitation of that tragic group of maimed and deformed women called "the Hiroshima Maidens." The atomic bomb that fell on that stricken city burned these girls so severely that they had lost whatever hopes they had for beauty and attractiveness. No man would marry them, they felt, and who would ever employ them? They were resigned to a life of invalidism and loneliness. Then an American newspaper editor realized the plight of these despairing girls and raised a sum of money to bring them to the United States and to the care of the finest plastic surgeons in the country. At Mount Sinai Hospital in New York they had several operations, and between surgery they were cared for lovingly by a group of Quakers. The effect of this love was more transforming than the effect of the surgeons' scalpel. As one of the girls was wheeled into the operating room she spoke in effect for them all: "Tell Dr. Barsky not to be worried because he cannot give me a new face. I know that this is impossible, but it does not matter; something has already healed here inside."

God spoke to Hosea through his domestic experience—and so now he speaks again. Have we created in our homes an opportunity for God to speak to us?

9

emergency entrants

Text: Acts 6:1-15; 7:55-60; 8:1

STEPHEN, THE FIRST CHRISTIAN MARTYR, MADE AN "EMER-gency entrance" into the Christian drama. Many of the Greek-speaking Jews, called Hellenists, were complaining that their widows did not receive as much pastoral attention as those of the old Jerusalem families. To meet this emergency demand for a larger staff the Apostles arranged for the election of seven promising young men to be the first deacons of the church, responsible for the distribution of relief to the needy, so as to relieve the Apostles' schedules in order that they might devote their full time to prayer, preaching, and teaching. The election of Stephen to meet this emergency gave no clue to his future role as a historic leader of the church.

The boy who is called off the bench to go into the football game never knows what destiny may await him. The worker who is transferred to a new department may be totally unaware that it will open up for him an exciting new career.

How many housewives have responded to the emergency need for someone to teach in the church school? They had no intention of ever becoming a prominent figure in the life of a church, and certainly no intention of becoming a major influence in the life of a growing personality. There was a job to be done and a lack of hands to do it, so a housewife volunteered her services. She made an emergency entrance into the Christian movement, and thus God spoke to her under circumstances similar to those in which he spoke to Stephen.

God calls many of us into ultimate significance from the ranks of the emergency entrants.

God Called Stephen into Significance Through the Emergency Entrance—And so Now He Speaks Again.

Many a life is wasted because it never faced a real challenge. The following advertisement ran in San Francisco newspapers in March, 1860:

WANTED: Men, young, sturdy, wiry fellows—not under 18; must be expert riders willing to risk death daily. Orphans preferred. Wages—$25.00 per week. Apply Central Overland Express.

History records that there were many answers to that ad. Young men who had been wasting their lives in the saloons of frontier communities responded to the challenge of the Pony Express. Their lives were just waiting for a real challenge.

How many youngsters would have wasted their talents

during the years of the great depression had not the Civilian Conservation Corps taken them off the streets into the mountains and into real opportunities for service to their country? As we contemplate the present social scene, with so many dropouts from school—youngsters untrained for any job forming into corner gangs—we wonder how many of these lads could be salvaged if they were ever confronted with a real challenge?

Again and again it has been demonstrated that men measure up to the magnitude of the task that faces them. The draftee whose top sergeant calls him "coward" may turn out in combat to be one of the bravest soldiers. The student who fails in early academic pursuits may in later life rise to the challenge of supporting a family and become an earnest seeker for truth in some research capacity. The whole panorama of human history vouches for the fact that, as well as making their times, men are made by their times.

Albert Schweitzer sat at his desk in France one evening reading a tract on the French mission in Africa. First he chucked it into the wastebasket. Then he retrieved it and continued reading. He became obsessed with a new vision as he read, and finally he exclaimed, "My search is over. At last I have found a job that is big enough!"

A prominent doctor was asked why he happened to choose medicine as a career. "As a small boy my younger brother took very ill," he replied. "The doctor was sent for and came as fast as horse and buggy could transport him. As the doctor entered I hid behind the sofa on which my brother lay. Here I observed my anxious parents and the country doctor with knitted brows hovering over my sick brother. Finally the doctor arose and said, 'You need not worry, the child will get well.' A heavenly light which was wonderful to behold fell across the faces of my parents. I decided then, as a child, to bring this light to the faces of others through service in medicine." God spoke to this boy through the experience of an emergency that made a claim upon him for the rest of his life.

We rarely recognize the moment that the door to greatness opens, for its hinges seldom squeak. "How silently, how silently the wondrous gift is given!" The chance date which eventuates in a gloriously happy marriage gives no indication of the wonderful things it holds in store. A casual shipboard acquaintance with a traveler may open up doorways of experience in another land that represent a turning point in our own attitudes. These opportune moments which pull us in new directions oftentimes become the signal for us to enter a whole new orbit.

Several years ago when I was busy at the task of erecting a new church building I received a letter from the bishop to the official board of my church, requesting the loan of my services for two weeks to the Methodist churches in Hawaii to assist in an island-wide campaign of preaching and visitation. I did not feel that I should go at that particular time. Neither did I see how I could fairly ask the church to pay my way on this mission when they were involved in heavy expenditures for construction. With the wisdom characteristic of women, however, my wife reminded me that I could not give a "vest pocket veto" to a letter from the bishop. I conveyed the message to the board chairman with the remark that this was a fine opportunity for service but scarcely possible at this time. To my amazement, however, he discussed it with the board, and they decided that any church that could afford 150,000 dollars for a new building could surely afford 300 dollars to send their pastor on a missionary assignment. Little did I know when I stepped aboard the plane that a year later I would be boarding another plane to embark upon a resident ministry in Hawaii. A doorway was opening before me, but I did not sense it at that time.

Just before takeoff pilots of jet planes receive instructions concerning the weather ahead. Sometimes it is necessary for them to fly several hundred miles out of the way to circumvent a storm. The interesting fact is that these apparent detours occasionally bring their flight to its destination ahead of schedule, for the same atmospheric disturbance that would provide head winds at the center of the storm may furnish tail winds on its perimeter to hasten the high flying craft on its way. Life's detours are not necessarily obstructions. The emergency that arises may mark the emergence of a great new opportunity.

God Spoke More Audibly Through Stephen's Quiet Deeds Than Through His Reasoned Words—And so Now He Speaks Again.

Stephen's sermon did not impress Saul! It was a good enough sermon tracing the history of God's dealings with the Jews. Nothing that Stephen said, however, changed Saul's opinion in the slightest degree, for the book of Acts states that "Saul was consenting to his death." The one thing that did impress Saul was the spirit in which Stephen died.

Have you ever noticed the difference in the ability of persons to make either poetry or scripture "come alive" for you? There are those who simply repeat it or read it, but there are others who not only interpret it, but also make you seem to feel it. Jesus commanded the attention of the congregation in the synagogue because he taught "as one who had authority, and not as the scribes." It was the quality of Jesus' life that illumined the words which he spoke. Missionaries have long since learned to take evangelism out "on location" if they are going to reach the people for the Christian faith. The missionary first builds a hospital to heal the sick or establishes a school to answer the questions of seeking minds. Later, when the people ask him why he came thus to serve them, he finds his opportunity to declare his faith. More impressive than words are the deeds of a Christian man. The world is more affected by practicing than by preaching.

As a deacon responsible for the distribution of relief funds Stephen found this social work to be a springboard for Christian witness to others. Many more persons can be reached by a demonstration of love and concern than by sermons, lectures, and tracts. In Calexico, California, a town on the Mexican border, there is a community center called "Neighborhood House." Church workers conduct a program of clubs for youth, a supervised playground for children, and a well-baby clinic for mothers. No attempt is made to teach the Bible. To do so would result in the suicide of the entire work, for Roman Catholic priests would never permit their Mexican parishioners to enroll in a Protestant training center. It is not necessary for the social workers at Neighborhood House to talk about the Bible, however. They simply live the Bible every day by their demonstrated love and concern for the forgotten immigrants along the border.

In the heart of downtown Honolulu stands the Nuuanu Y.M.C.A. Ministering in the most crowded section of the city, the Nuuanu Y forces no religious program down the throats of reluctant youth from non-Christian homes. It simply demonstrates the Christian religion by taking an interest in hundreds of boys and girls who would otherwise fall into street gangs and go through life never knowing what it is to be loved and trained into leadership. Out of the lanes and alleys of the most impoverished section of Honolulu have come multitudes of youth who have gradually opened their lives to the church because they were first taught the meaning of love and care for them as individuals by Y leaders who gave them their time and affection. This social program has proved to be the springboard from which many young lives have plunged into their first contact with the Christian religion and into the life of the church. The day always comes when youngsters begin to wonder why their leaders spend so much time with them and why they sprout gray hairs in their behalf. Then they understand that the motivation for care and service comes from the Christian's experience of a God who first cared for us. To preach first and practice afterwards is to put the cart before the horse.

Few are called to preach, but many are called to practice.

God Spoke to Stephen Through the Emergency Rations of His Memories—And so Now He Speaks Again.

Oscar Wilde once said, "Alas, I am dying beyond my means." Stephen did not die beyond his means, for he discovered the infinite resources of God. So common was this resource to the early Christians that their Roman persecutors were impelled to write of them, "These Christians die well!"

Dying "within our means" is possible only when we are aware of the infinite spiritual resources which Christ offers to us. Not long ago a man who had been a beggar all his life received word that he had been left a fortune of several hundred thousand dollars. His surprise was no greater than the amazement that overcomes the Christian when, in the midst of trial and tribulation, he discovers "the unsearchable riches of Christ" that insure him against every emergency. Words come to his lips in a crisis that he never thought of before. Strength flows into him from no visible source, yet it visibly strengthens him to withstand the attempts of his tormentors to brainwash him. From the days of the martyrs to the Christians who stood up under imprisonment and torture during the recent wars, men have read a New Testament in the lives of those whose behavior betrays the fact that they have seen Jesus.

Stephen was sustained in the hour of his stoning by the memory of his Lord stretched upon the cross. So intensely had Stephen contemplated this memory that when he found himself in a similar position of torment he found the same words rising to his lips that came to those of Christ. "Lord, do not hold this sin against them."

We are largely sustained by our memories. If we remember only the dark and evil deeds we have done in the past we will develop a sense of guilt and inferiority. If, however, in our old age we remember the happy scenes of the past we can face life with brightness despite the onward creeping of physical infirmity. If we are rich with memories of our experiences with the presence of God we find emergency rations to sustain us in every trial.

Sometimes on mountain highways we come upon large mirrors set by the roadside to enable us to see around the curves ahead. So the lives of Christians like Stephen reflect the God we cannot yet see. This is the Holy Spirit that Christ promised would reprieve us from sin and sustain us in tribulations.

The short life of Stephen seems a terrific waste—but was it? That which is short and deep has the same content as that which is long and shallow. The gravestones of our American revolutionaries reveal that most of them died as young men, but would you say that they died in vain? Jesus lived to be only thirty-three and preached for only three years, yet that short life has become the turning point for human history.

"It is to your advantage that I go away," Jesus said to his disciples. If Stephen's death so impressed Saul that it turned him into Paul the apostle and launched him on his great missionary career, then Stephen did not live in vain. If the young medical researcher was poisoned by his own experiment and gave "his life as a ransom for many" then he did not live in vain. If by losing my life I enable others to find life then I have discovered God's purpose for my life—even if it appeared to be death.

Stephen was called for in emergency and died in emergency, but for this hour he came into the world. Can we, then know in advance the purpose of our true calling? Perhaps we are all emergency entrants in the drama of life.

10
breaking through the crust

Text: Acts 6; 7:55-60; 8:1a

DO YOU KNOW ANYONE WHO SEEMS TO BE A HOPELESS CASE?
Is there in your acquaintance an individual whom you have
often tried to reach with a challenge but who never seems
to respond to your efforts? Perhaps it is an alcoholic in the
family. Perhaps it is a youth with a high potential for leadership who simply refuses to study. Perhaps it is a religiously
indifferent friend whom you have invited to church repeatedly but who remains frankly disinterested. If your inability to reach these hopeless cases frustrates you, how
much more must God be frustrated by our free will as we
persistently refuse his love and his way? After all, he loves
us far more than we can love any other human being, and
he has so many more persons to frustrate him than we do!

Such a person was Saul of Tarsus. He was a brilliant
young man with a tremendous potential for dynamic leadership. The amazing results which he was subsequently able

to accomplish as the first missionary to the Gentiles indicates the enormous capacity for leadership which this man possessed. How God must have longed to reach him, but for years Saul persisted in having his own way and in hardening his heart against the call to the Christian faith. He was a man of completely misdirected zeal, persecuting the Christians with a fanatically misplaced devotion, and God found it impossible to reach him through the preaching of the Apostles. Then God found one line of communication still open into Saul's heart—the death and awe-inspiring influence of Stephen. As the blows struck his body Stephen cried aloud, "Lord Jesus, receive my spirit," and lifted his eyes toward heaven with a smile of exaltation. As his knees buckled under him in the waning moments of his life he displayed a capacity for forgiveness that Saul had never seen among his legalistic friends, for the young martyr cried out in the tradition of his Master, "Lord, do not hold this sin against them." The memory of Stephen's death burned into the soul of Saul, and though the young martyr's own life was cut short he threw a shadow that lengthened across history in the life of the man who saw him die. God found an open channel into the hardened heart of Saul through the life of another man, and so now he speaks again to hardened hearts through the witness of others' lives.

God Awakened Life in One Man Through the Death of Another—And so Now He Speaks Again.

Sholem Asch, the Jewish biographer, gave us a very likely psycho-study of Paul in his classic *The Apostle*. It is his thesis that as Saul journeyed northward along the road to

Damascus for a further pogrom of the Christians his mind's eye smarted with a memory of the radiant face and the amazing, undeserved love of the dying Stephen. At last he had met his equal in devotion and zeal, and as the burning sun beat down upon his head and his mind was obsessed with the memory of the young martyr, the radiance of the latter's face combined with the brilliance of the desert to blind him. In that moment for the first time he realized that he had been persecuting the true Christ.

A man's shadow may be so lengthened by his death that he measures most in the hour when he lives last. In Lloyd C. Douglas' great novel *The Magnificent Obsession* the story is told of a rather worthless young playboy named Bobby Merrick who is rescued from drowning while an eminent brain surgeon, Wayne Hudson, perishes for lack of a pulmotor. When young Merrick regains consciousness in the hospital he overhears the words of the chief nurse who is mourning the passing of the great brain surgeon in favor of this worthless young spendthrift. It occurs to her that if he wanted to Bobby might study surgery and try to take the place of the man who lost his life saving him. "He'd never do it, of course," she mused. "Couldn't . . . wouldn't . . . it would be too hard . . . take too long . . . but God! . . . what a chance!" Young Merrick heard her words as a challenge to his inmost soul, and he became Dr. Hudson's replacement.

One of the spiritual discoveries of our time is the rising popularity of the devotional literature composed by Dietrich Bonhoeffer, the German martyr who died in a Nazi concentration camp because he would not renounce the supreme sovereignty of God. If Bonhoeffer had lived he would have been an effective pastor, and his preaching might have inspired thousands. By his death for the Christian cause, however, Dietrich Bonhoeffer has become one of the great heroes of the faith, and his books have reached thousands beyond the limits of his voice. Through his death many have found a deeper spiritual life than they would ever have known otherwise. So now he speaks again—even to our own generation!

A sophisticated college student was lounging against a pillar in the stadium as a speaker delivered a Memorial Day address. He was not particularly interested in the subject matter until a remark in the address startled him to a new spiritual awareness. Suddenly, the question stabbed through the student's mind like a knife: "Am I worth dying for?" He realized the awful waste of talent and personality that had been sacrificed in all of the wars of our country to this hour, and then he realized that he was the survivor who must justify the sacrifices of all his forbears. They thus spoke to him in death as they might not have reached him in life.

It is not death that is tragedy—it is insignificance that is tragedy!

God "Broke Through" to Saul Through a Challenging Life —And so Now He Speaks Again.

Some who won't listen to God directly may be willing to listen to an echo of his voice in the example of someone else. A pompous bishop, touring India to question the confirmation classes, came to a class taught by a missionary named Murray. He asked the students what it was to be a

Christian. A little Indian boy raised his hand and said, "It is to live like Mr. Murray!"

For many years the laymen in the church in which I was reared tried to persuade my father to join the church. He was always polite when they called but always firmly refused to join. Then one Sunday he startled everyone by walking down the aisle to take the vows of membership. Someone asked him which one of the callers had been successful in persuading him to join. He replied, "I did not join the church because of the persuasion of any caller. I joined the church because my wife showed me in her own life that it really makes a difference!"

Everyone has heard of Augustine, the author of *The City of God*, but not everyone has heard that he was not always a saint. As a youth he was a libertine, anxious to get away from home and family traditions. He rebelled against the church; he went off to North Africa in quest of adventure. His wise mother, Monica, did not argue with the youth, but quietly wrote a letter to Bishop Ambrose of Alexandria requesting him to befriend and take an interest in her boy. Years later Augustine wrote of this influence, "I began to love him, not at first as a teacher of truth, which I despaired of finding in the church, but as a fellow creature who was kind to me." Augustine was won to Christianity not by a theological argument but by the sincere friendship of Ambrose.

To somebody you are a hero—to your son, to your daughter, to your wife or sweetheart, to someone under your command, to the pupil, or to the boy down the street. Your life is influencing someone for good or for ill.

102

Do not discount the bystander. He may be your silent partner. Stephen did not realize as he crumpled in death that the man who held the cloaks for those who threw the stones at him would actually become his own successor in the gospel and would carry it to limits of which he never dreamed. The most significant contribution of your life may be in the example that you have set before an observer whom you may not even know. Though your marriage may have failed, though your children may be long gone, though your hopes for a career may have ended disastrously, you are not a failure if your example has launched a significant life.

When one has no key to the front door he tries the back door. If all the doors are closed he tries a window. So does God! He speaks directly to some, but to others he must make oblique approaches. Jesus touched persons who had been completely unmoved by the preaching of John the Baptist. Billy Graham will appeal to one man, while Ralph Sockman will appeal to another. This is the value of the so-called itinerant ministry in The Methodist Church. Each pastor who comes to serve a congregation brings a different personality and different talents. If pastors do not stay too long a greater number of persons will be touched by the diverse skills of successive men.

Some persons responded when Jesus said, "Come and follow." Others responded as did Andrew when his brother simply said to him, "Come and see." There is more than one way to break through the crust of a closed heart, and God will conspire to open these channels as we make ourselves available to him.

God Kept Tooling Away at Saul's Hardened Heart—And so Now He Speaks Again.

Do you ever marvel at the infinite patience of God as we close our ears against his call? How many times have men stumbled into blind-alley jobs in which they found no joy and no sense of satisfaction because they insisted on following their own wills or the opportunism of the moment? Many a square peg has found himself in a round hole because he refused to follow the leadership of his heart. God tries to guide us, but we listen only to our own voices instead of to his. "How often would I have gathered [you] . . . and you would not," said the Master.

If you are discouraged about your inability to get through to your own family remember that Jesus was unable to win the immediate following of any of his brothers and sisters. Sometime later, however, his brother James became the great leader of the church in Jerusalem. Granite is slower to quarry than chalk, but it is much more durable. The person with the hardest crust may be the most productive if we allow enough time for the penetration of that crust.

The Christian churches in Hawaii have discovered that the methods of decision effective on the mainland are ineffective among the orientals of Buddhist background in the islands. I participated in a preaching mission in a church in a plantation community. Every year someone had done a preaching mission in that church. Every year the same people from that town attended the special services as a courtesy to the visiting guest. Yet none responded directly to my invitation to accept Christian discipleship. Over succeeding months and years, however, the people of this town one by one committed themselves to the church and became the most dynamic of Christians. I learned this lesson in Hawaii: Those who make rapid decisions do not necessarily abide by their decisions, while those who may be slow to decide will be sure when they decide.

God spoke to Saul through a chorus of many different voices rather than through one solo voice. He spoke to his devotion through the personal teachings of Rabbi Gamaliel. He spoke to his faith through the example of the dying Stephen. Without the influence of Gamaliel Paul could never have reasoned out the theology which made him an effective missionary to the philosophically trained Gentiles. Without the memory and the example of Stephen he would never have found the faith that justifies when actions are inadequate.

We think of John Wesley's heartwarming experience in the chapel on Aldersgate Street in London, May 24, 1738, as the turning point in his life. Have we stopped to consider, however, that at least eight ingredients went into the context of that experience?

1. The Bible, which Wesley opened to the words: "Whereby are given unto us exceeding great and precious promises: that by these ye might be partakers of the divine nature." (II Pet. 1:4 K.J.V.)

2. A friend who invited Wesley to go with him that night to Saint Paul's, though Wesley was rather reluctant.

3. A great cathedral he had entered and in which he had worshiped that morning.

4. A choir singing an anthem from the Ps. 130: "Out of the depths have I cried unto thee, O Lord."

5. A little group of people praying in an upper room.

6. A clergyman named Martin Luther, whose "Preface to the Epistle to the Romans" was being read.

7. A layman—the person who was probably reading that commentary that evening.

8. The power of the Holy Spirit warming his heart.

This means that God is not only speaking to you through others, but he is also speaking through you to others. The closing scene of *The Diary of Anne Frank* shows the father, Otto Frank, as he returns to the Amsterdam garret in which his family and another Jewish family had hidden for four years during the Nazi occupation. He is reading the diary of his teen-age daughter who died in a concentration camp, and he chokes up as he comes to the line, "In spite of everything, I still believe that there is good in everyone." "She puts me to shame," exclaims her father as he collapses into a chair. So does everyone who lives his religion even more than he speaks it.

Like a mirror you can reflect light into an otherwise darkened corner—but only by facing the Light yourself!

You can reach into the hardened hearts that will not respond directly to God, but you can do so only by turning your own life constantly toward God.

The only line of communication opened to a hardened heart is the reflection of God in a dedicated life. This was the meaning of Stephen's transfiguration. Your life is still a summons, for as once he spoke to Saul through Stephen, so now he speaks again through you!

11

the man behind the boy

Text: Acts 4:32-37; 13:1-3; 15:1-2, 12, 22, 36-39; Gal. 2: 9-13

AFTER A MALE BABY HAS GROWN OUT OF LONG CLOTHES AND triangles and has acquired pants, freckles and so much dirt that relatives dare not kiss it between meals, it becomes a . . . boy. A boy's nature answers to that false belief that there is no such thing as perpetual motion. A boy can swim like a fish, run like a deer, climb like a squirrel, balk like a mule, bellow like a bull, eat like a pig or act like a jackass according to climatic conditions!

He is a piece of skin stretched over an appetite, a noise covered with smudges. He is called a tornado because he comes in at the most unexpected place, and leaves everything a wreck behind him. He is a growing animal of superlative promise to be watered and kept warm, a joy forever, a periodic nuisance, the problem of our times, the hope of a nation. Every new boy born is evidence that God is not yet discouraged at man.

Were it not for boys, the newspapers would go unread, and a thousand picture shows would go bankrupt. Boys are useful in running errands with the aid of five or six adults. The zest with which a boy does an errand is equaled only by the speed of a turtle on a July day. The boy is a natural spectator. He watches parades, fires, fights, ball games, automobiles, boats and airplanes with equal fervor, but will not watch the clock. The man who invents a clock that will stand on its head and sing a song while it strikes, will win the undying gratitude of millions of families whose boys are forever coming home to lunch around dinner time.

Boys faithfully imitate their dads in spite of all efforts to teach them manners! A boy, if not washed too often and if kept in a cool, dirty place after each accident, will survive broken bones, hornets, swimming holes, fights, and nine helpings of pie.

There is always a man behind the boy. Every youth has his hero! It may be his father; it may be his scoutmaster; it may be his Y leader; it may be a counselor; it may be his teacher; it may be a movie star; or it may be the man next door. But every youth has a dream realized in human flesh that walks before him.

It was so with young John Mark, the chronicler of the first gospel. The man behind this boy was his cousin Barnabas.

God Called Mark into a Life of Service by Attracting Him to a "Boy's Man"—And so Now He Speaks Again.

We hear a lot about a "man's man" and about a "lady's man," but there is also a "boy's man." There are certain qualities, however, which must characterize the life of a boy's man. He must lead an exciting life—one which will be glamourous to the heart of a young dreamer to challenge the best that is in him. Barnabas, the Cypriot traveler, led exactly such a life. Coming from the fabled cities to the north and west, he brought into the provincial home in Jerusalem a breath of exciting experiences and adventures that intrigued young Mark.

A boy's man must be genuine, for no one in the world can spot a phony quicker than a lad. When Mark saw Barnabas bring in the entire sum of money he had realized from the sale of some land and deposit it in the common treasury of the early church the lad knew that he had found a sincere man who really practiced what he preached.

Finally, a boy's man must show an interest in youth, not simply polite and academic attention but willingness to share a part of his life and time with a youth. Barnabas did exactly this; he was willing to include Mark in his conversation and in his future plans. Nothing is more disgusting to an intelligent youth than adults who enter the home for a visit and deliberately exclude the youth from the conversation. Barnabas must have talked to Mark extensively to have aroused his interest in accompanying his cousin on his journey. He was willing to include Mark as a member of his traveling party, despite the eccentricities that always characterize teen-agers in unfamiliar surroundings. Furthermore, Barnabas understood Mark's changing moods, and every teen-ager is like the Hawaiian sky—ever changing. Barnabas understood Mark as quickly when he wanted to go home as he did when he wanted to go away. Only a man with the kind of understanding that can feel with a boy's heart can ever be a boy's man.

Such a man can become a real influence on a youth. "I

was born," said Sir Henry Jones, "in Langernyew in 1852 and born again in Edward Caird's classroom in 1876." Who has not had his imagination kindled and his mind stirred by some beloved teacher? Teachers influence young lives most.

I remember a young man who was asked to teach a church-school class of intermediate boys. He was not contented simply to teach them the regular lessons but wanted to mold their character by more frequent contact. He took them out to play football on Saturday afternoons and spent part of his leisure evenings diagraming new plays for the boys to learn. He gave up his Friday evenings to work with a coeducational club of junior highs, taking them to the skating rinks, on hikes and picnics, to the beach, and to parties. This man came to have a profound influence on the lives of the seventy-five youngsters in that group.

Jim, a village carpenter in an Indiana town, always started down the main street to church on Sunday morning promptly at 9:15 A.M., for he wanted to be on time for Sunday school. The villagers had learned they could set their clocks by his regular trips. Jim wasn't an orator, could not sing a solo, and never went on visitation campaigns. He was just a quiet Christian who went to church every Sunday, come rain, come blizzard, or come shine. One of the so-called "wild" young fellows at the village tavern was once heard to remark, "If I ever become a Christian I want to be like Old Jim." During the next Easter season this same young man did join the church. What changed him? It was the example of loyal Old Jim plodding down the street at exactly 9:15 each Sunday morning. One never knows how many youthful lives are being touched by a life of simple integrity.

Who are the boy's men in your community? I suspect they are the scoutmasters, the youth-group counselors, and a host of admired laymen in civic life and leadership. Perhaps they are like the man who had a little shop for the repairing of musical instruments next to his humble home, and who made it his business to teach school children how to appreciate the best in music. The man behind the boy may well be one like him.

God Encouraged Mark Through a Man Who Would Rather Lose His Job Than to Lose a Boy. And so Now He Speaks Again.

It seemed a pity to break up a great team, but Barnabas preferred oblivion to seeing Mark's self-confidence destroyed. It would have been wonderful to go on with Paul to a distinguished missionary career, but it would have been tragic to leave behind a lad with so much promise. In choosing between the company of a great man and a boy with a great future, Barnabas chose the boy.

It can often be costly to stand by a "bad-risk" youth. A judge in Honolulu recently took that kind of stand. He stated that it was more important to rehabilitate than to punish a wayward youth. Scores of newspaper readers wrote letters of protest against him, and he lost much popularity. He would rather lose support than to lose a boy, however.

Don't ever give up on a youth. That's what produces gangsters! Some years ago a boy whose mother had died was growing up alone in a little Indiana town. Nobody had

111

any time or affection for him, and nobody seemed to care what happened to him. He attended Sunday school rather indifferently, but even there nobody seemed to care much about him as an individual. They were more interested in what he did to the group than in what the group could do for him. Soon he had committed some minor juvenile crime and was sent away to reform school. When he came back home he intended to go straight. The little church where he had attended Sunday school was holding evangelistic services, and he went. He responded to the altar call to dedicate his life to the Christian way, but afterwards there was no hand of affection laid on his shoulder and no word of encouragement offered. Nobody seemed to care; even the minister seemed skeptical. Is it any wonder that he didn't stick it out? He began to drift from bad to worse, and in the end made a nation shudder as America's Public Enemy No. 1 until his body was riddled with policemen's bullets. That boy was John Dillinger.

As Mark needed a "standby," so do confused youths today. In Owen Wister's book *The Virginian* the uncultured cowboy who had been lifted by human love said, "It was neither preaching nor praying that made a better man of me, but one or two people who believed in me better than I deserved, and I hated to disappoint them."

Some thirty years ago a class in sociology at Johns Hopkins University made a scientific study of one of the worst slum districts of Baltimore. The students went into homes, interviewed parents and children, and noted good and bad influences in each case. They tabulated the results on cards. Two hundred cards were marked "headed for jail," and on each card was the name of a boy or a girl whose environment and attitudes indicated a future life of crime. After a lapse of twenty-five years another sociology class in Johns Hopkins found this bundle of cards marked "headed for jail" and decided to take as their year's project a check on every individual name. To their utter amazement they discovered that only two persons on the cards marked "headed for jail" ever got there. The reason was "Aunt Hannah," a teacher in the grade school of that particular slum section. The stories of the two hundred ran true to the same pattern. One man said, "I sure was a bad egg. I was the worst kid in the neighborhood, and how the cops did like to pin any and everything on me! And they were usually right. Then one day Aunt Hannah kept me after school. She told me I was too smart a kid to be getting into trouble, and before I left she asked me to come to her home for dinner the next Sunday. I just never had the heart to let Aunt Hannah down after that, and now I'm a doctor in this same community."

God Voiced His Confidence in a Youth Through an Older Man's Recollections—And so Now He Speaks Again.

Paul was perfectly right that Mark had once proved untrustworthy, but Barnabas was unwilling to hold one mistake against him. Perhaps it was because Barnabas, like Mark, had also been a disappointment once to perfectionist Paul. Paul described in Gal. 2:13 the time when Barnabas was "carried away" by segregationist pressure in Antioch. Having thus slipped once he was very tolerant of Mark's human error.

113

Moses, David, and Peter each slipped once too. Moses lost his temper; David was guilty of adultery; Peter denied his Lord in a moment of cowardice. God didn't give them up! It is quite true that Moses' temper cost him the privilege of entering the Promised Land. It is quite true that David's bitter remorse and Peter's shattered self-confidence hurt them as long as they lived. But all three of these men did great things for God after the day of their sin—even as Mark and Barnabas, and you and I.

The story is told that there was once an artist who worked long and hard but his paintings were only ordinary. He lacked the spark of genius to produce great art. From sheer exhaustion he fell asleep one day beside his work. As he slept a great artist entered his studio and added the few extra touches which turned a mediocre work into a masterpiece. God can do that same thing with such imperfect material as Mark and Barnabas, and you and I.

God still had a place for Barnabas on a new team— training youth with his patience! "Not good enough" is an alibi, not a release from responsibility. Some of the greatest contributions to human life have come from men whose past records were tarnished. This is the real assurance that comes to you and me as we remember the faith that Barnabas had in Mark and the gospel that the latter left as a lasting legacy.

Behind every youth there stands a man. It may or may not be his father. Where are you standing—behind a youth, or in his way?

12

tracing God's signature

Text: Rev. 1:9-11; 2:8-11

WE HAVE BEEN OBSERVING THE DIVERSE WAYS IN WHICH
God speaks to persons. Going through the Bible from
Genesis to Revelation, we have observed various biblical
personalities as types of the different ways by which God
speaks to the heart of man. Now we come to the final and
most difficult to understand of all these ways—the process
of revelation.

There come times in our lives when God's ways seem
to be beyond human understanding. These are the times
when he seems to have deserted his children and gone
off indifferent to their fate. Prisoners in concentration
camps might find it difficult to believe in a historical God
who actually cares about what happens to human beings in
daily events. Persons in the arena of conflict between the
forces of honesty and dishonesty or of justice and injustice
are quick to sense the times when they see "right forever
on the scaffold, wrong forever on the throne." The businessman who has lost valuable contracts to an unscrupulous

competitor, the colored person who is denied opportunity to live in a nice neighborhood because of the color of his skin, the honest statesman who is rejected at the polls by an electorate that blindly follows an unscrupulous politician—each of these has reason to wonder if Christ is still the lord of history. It is then that we need help in tracing God's signature in current events.

It was for such an hour that the revelation of John was given to us. This final book in the New Testament was written by a figure known as John of Patmos—not to be confused with John the disciple. During the reign of the Roman Emperor Domitian an image of the emperor was placed in every courtroom, and Christians were arrested, brought into the courtroom, and given the alternative of bowing down in worship before the emperor or professing their faith in the Lordship of the Christ and being fed to the lions. John belonged to the latter company, but instead of being sent to the arena he was exiled to the lonely island of Patmos off the present coast of Turkey. There God spoke to him—not in a trance, but in an insight—and so now he speaks again.

God Spoke to the Victims of Evil in Roman Times Through the Pen of a Contemporary—And so Now He Speaks Again.

"Misery loves company." You would rather visit with an individual who has had your illness and can discuss its symptoms and pains sympathetically than with anyone else. A mother having difficulty with her children would rather discuss her problem with another mother than to

116

read the advice of the best-trained childless authority on earth. No barrier is more dangerous to missionary work than the difference in experience that sometimes exists between the missionary who wishes to export his American comforts and living standards and the underprivileged person whom he feels called to serve. There is no substitute for experience.

A minister friend of mine served a church in a little town adjacent to the state mental hospital. Once a month it was his custom to preach at the asylum, and the patients came to know him quite well. One afternoon after his sermon an old lady approached him wreathed in smiles. "Oh, Reverend Carlson, she said, "we do look forward so much to your coming. Somehow, you seem just like one of us." That was intended to be a compliment!

Because John of Patmos was able to say, " I John, your brother, who share with you . . . the tribulation," he won a hearing—then and now.

In his lonely isolation on a distant island he yearned to speak words of strength and comfort to his fellow Christians who were members of the churches in the seven largest cities of the Roman province of Asia—now West Asia Minor. But how could he get the message through? There were many miles of water and land between him and the seven congregations he yearned to address. By what possible means could the encouragement of God come to these Christians in their hour of persecution? Then he looked at his hands and realized that he could still grasp a pen in his fingers. No matter how far you may be from those you love or those you yearn to encourage, you can still write. The mail boat still runs!

Indeed, literature has proved itself across the centuries to be a major vehicle for the communication of ideals. In American Revolutionary times the pamphlets of Thomas Paine made the people think. During the movement for the abolition of slavery the novel *Uncle Tom's Cabin*, by Harriet Beecher Stowe, aroused the conscience of many thousands more than were aroused by the speeches of the most eloquent abolitionist politicians. Every library is an arsenal of ideas, and books have reached out to those beyond the reach of the human voice.

The church I attended as a teen-ager was located only half a block from the First Congregational Church of Los Angeles whose pastor at the time was Dr. Lloyd C. Douglas. Dr. Douglas led that church ably, but he faced some rather rough competition in adjoining pulpits which were blessed with speakers even more eloquent than he. Then Dr. Douglas realized that his genius lay in writing, and he retired from the preaching pulpit to reach a much vaster audience with his pen. His novels, such as *Magnificent Obsession, Green Light, The Robe,* and *The Big Fisherman,* have brought a Christian challenge to thousands who would never have darkened the door of his church. God speaks to many today through the pen of a contemporary, even as he spoke to the members of the churches of Asia through the pen of John of Patmos.

Indeed, today even new thought forms are becoming instruments for the communuication of God's thoughts. The radio and television ministry of the church provide a vivid means of reaching people effectively. The church now employs expert script writers to provide the best in drama and TV for nationwide broadcasts. Do not scorn the new testaments to faith which carry God's latest word to us. Remember that he speaks in different ways to different circumstances, and he may use a different instrument to reach your loved ones than he used to challenge you.

God Spoke to John Through an Understanding of History —And so Now He Speaks Again.

As he faced the totalitarian threat John refused to see the present hour out of context. He did not regard the latest clipping from the morning paper as indicative of God's desertion of his world. Rather, he insisted that this morning's clipping actually belonged in the context of the whole library of historical experience which had gone before. He therefore believed that the future was as trustworthy as was the past. In his exile and isolation John meditated upon the course of human history in the past. He asked himself what teams had won in past contests between good and evil, and he asked himself what were their training rules. The more he studied the record of human experience the more convinced he became that there was a direct relationship between the events on the earthly stage of life and the divine purposes on the heavenly stage. He saw the current hour in its larger perspective of the stream of eternity of which it was but one part. When he viewed the sufferings of the present hour against the larger backdrop of human history he realized that the days of the conqueror are always numbered, but that the meek had already inherited the earth. So he wrote his message of encouragement to his contemporaries in the form of a play that took place on two stages—an upper and a lower—and in four acts—Act I, evil supreme; Act II, evil challenged; Act III, evil checked; Act IV, evil banished.

The thought forms of the Revelation of John are difficult for moderns to understand, but they are not so difficult when put in their historical setting. Remember that the Greek drama which was so familiar in those times often depicted activities on two stages, the upper representing the gods of heaven and the lower representing the mortals of earth. In his historical drama John keeps changing his focus from the doleful events on earth to the strategy in heaven. Furthermore, he was under the necessity of writing his drama in code in order to pass censorship. This is no new experience to us. During World War II when it was forbidden for servicemen to write their families where they were stationed lest troop movements be betrayed to the enemy it was commonplace for families to agree in advance on code words in letters that would reveal the destinations of their sons. If the letter asked about Aunt Frances it meant that he had gone to France. If he asked about Uncle Jake it might mean that he had gone to Japan.

In like manner the early Christians devised a code among themselves. Rome was known as the city of seven hills, so whenever reference was made to the number seven the early Christians knew that it referred to Rome. The four corners of the compass were often referred to as the four corners of the earth—which was then considered to be flat. Hence reference to four or multiples thereof referred to things earthly. God had chosen twelve tribes of Israel and Christ had chosen twelve disciples, so the number twelve and its multiples became the symbol of things heavenly. God had created the earth in seven periods, so the number seven was sometimes also used as a symbol of completion. All these things make mysterious reading for modern eyes, but they constitute an allegory that was readily decoded by the early Christians, although incomprehensible to their Roman persecutors. As this strangely visionary book cir culated among the churches it reminded them that the sufferings of the moment were only a small scene in the human drama and that the ultimate purposes of God— from the upperstage—would yet prevail. Revelation, then, is a philosophy of history, a proclamation of faith that God is the lord of history and will always see that ultimately the righteous triumph upon the earth while evil vanishes from the scene.

That is why it is hard to brainwash a Christian—he has a heritage of certainty! The Chinese Reds discovered that it was relatively easy to brainwash American prisoners of war who had no religious depth, but they found it quite impossible to erase the faith of those who saw all current events against the larger backdrop of God's eternal purposes.

That is why the Norwegian Christians refused to yield to the demands of Hitler in World War II. That is why Martin Niemöller was able to defy the dictates of the Fuehrer with Luther's hymn "A mighty fortress is our God" upon his lips. That is why the prisoners of the Japanese in Singapore never despaired as they looked up through the barred windows of their cell and saw the cross atop the spire of Wesley Methodist Church across the street. That is why a group of missionaries on the famed Korean death march never lost their faith in ultimate victory and deliverance.

Headlines will yellow with age, but righteousness will always live. That is the glory and truth of the motto of the Hawaiian royalty which has since become the motto of the state of Hawaii: "The life of the land is preserved in righteousness."

God Spoke to John Through an Insight into the Future— And so Now He Speaks Again.

John of Patmos saw history as a dual controlled vehicle. You have seen the driver education cars in which students are taught to drive. The student is in complete control of the car, but the vehicle is equipped against finality by another control available to the instructor in the event of impending tragedy. This was John's concept of history, that through our free will we control the course of human destiny but that we do not have a monopoly upon history because God is seated beside us as an insurance against the total finality of our own stupidity or depravity. There is an arena for free will in our lives, but evil can't get off limits. That is why John was able to say, "Do not fear what you are about to suffer." He knew it couldn't last. He remembered the history of the Jews in Egypt, in Babylon, and against countless enemies. He remembered the victory of Jesus after three dark days. So, although he reminded his persecuted friends that they might have to suffer for ten days—with the possibility that other zeroes might be added for an indeterminate period—yet he knew that the days of evil were

122

definitely numbered while the days of righteousness are eternal. So his drama unfolded through the four acts of the historical process as he saw it: Evil supreme, evil challenged, evil checked, and evil vanquished. There is, therefore, no cause for panic in Red threats nor H-bomb scares. The sands of the dark hour will run out, but the sun of righteousness will rise again!

Four men were standing in a telegraph office while a message was being received. Three of them heard merely a succession of taps. The other surprised his companions by repeating the message aloud. He knew the code.

Any economist knows that business forecasting is not a matter of clairvoyance; it is an analytical observation. The economist who has carefully studied the ups and downs of past business cycles can read the signs of the times by making a careful analysis of such factors as price levels, inventories, car loadings, and mortgage foreclosures. A careful analysis of the facts enables him to foretell the future.

In like manner, the vision of John is neither a psychic prophecy nor a wish-thinking dream. It is a spelling out of the facts of the historical process, enabling the faithful to ascertain their position in the cycle of suffering.

Herein lies the tragedy of unread adults and of unrooted children. The man or woman who is ignorant of the Bible and of the story of God's activities in human history is at the mercy of the daily headlines, but one who is rooted firmly in his faith can by a study of God's past dealings with men face the worst tragedy unflinchingly. What a tragedy that when such a faith is available to us we shall fail to take advantage of it! Why do we spend more time reading the headlines than the Bible? Why do we deliberately choose to ignore the heritage of our faith and want to talk about and discuss anything and everything else under the sun except God's purposes for human life? The parent who denies to his children that legacy of confidence in the God of history is sending them forth into the world unequipped to face frustration and tragedy, and this is an inexcusable robbery of childhood. As once God spoke to John through an understanding of history so now he speaks again to us if we will take the time to read and to think. That is why John says to us: "He who has an ear, let him hear."

Henry Clay, the American statesman, was once crossing the Appalachian Mountains. During a rest period he put his ear to the ground listening intently. To his companions, who asked what he was about, he explained, "I hear the tramp of coming millions!" If we have historical sensitivity we are not bound by the restrictions of the times in which we live, but we see everything that happens today against the larger background of past experience and future trend. What Henry Clay foresaw for the American West the sensitive Christian can foresee in the course of human suffering.

God spoke to the victims of evil in Roman times through a man who could read between the lines of current history, and so now he speaks again. Have you learned to read thus —by insight as well as by eyesight? The church is here to enable you to do that very thing!